TESTIMONY:
DEATH OF A GUATEMALAN VILLAGE

By
Victor Montejo

Translated by Victor Perera

Curbstone Press

First published in cloth and paperback, 1987
Second printing in paperback, 1988
Third printing in paperback, 1991

Curbstone Press is a 501(c)(3) nonprofit literary arts
organization whose operations are supported in part
by private donations and by grants from the ADCO
Foundation, the Andrew W. Mellon Foundation, the
National Endowment for the Arts, the Plumsock Fund,
and the Connecticut Commission on the Arts, a State
Agency whose funds are recommended by the Governor
and appropriated by the State Legislature.

Photograph: Guatemalan refugees
in Chiapas, Mexico, November 1982
© 1983 Kenneth Silverman
Cover design by Stone Graphics

LC: 86-71063
ISBN: 0-915306-65-4

distributed by
INBOOK
P.O. Box 120470
East Haven, CT 06512

CURBSTONE PRESS, 321 Jackson St., Willimantic, CT 06226

acknowledgements

I wish to express my gratitude to Bonnie Poteet, Gene Chenoweth and John Peeler, Professors at Bucknell University and to Father John Coyne for being so helpful to me and my family during our residency in Lewisburg, Pennsylvania. Also I wish to express my thanks to all my friends who wish to remain anonymous, especially those who have been contributing to the Montejo Fund. I wish, too, to thank all my friends at SUNY, Gary Gossen and Professor Robert Carmack, and all the people who have contributed to my fellowship at SUNY. To all of them, many thanks for their solidarity.

Dedicatoria

Dedico este libro
a la memoria
de los muchos miles
de Guatemaltecos
muertos y desaparecidos
durante esta década
de agresión y de lucha.
Y, a pesar
de que se intente
olvidar sus nombres
poco a poco,
yo sé que flores silvestres
siguen brotando diariamente
de sus huesos clandestinos –
allá en barrancos y montañas.

Dedication

I dedicate this book
to the memory
of the many thousand
Guatemalans
who were killed or disappeared
during this decade
of aggression and struggle.
And even
if there are attempts
to blot out their names
little by little
I know that wild flowers
are growing daily
from their clandestine bones –
scattered there in the ravines and the mountains.

TESTIMONY:
DEATH OF A
GUATEMALAN
VILLAGE

PRELUDE

Tzalalá is a remote village in the northwest of Hue-huetenango Department in Guatemala, Central America. There are no movie houses nor theaters, television, electric light, drinking water or highways. The only access to this community is by narrow twisting roads that cross streams and deep gullies as they climb high into the craggy uplands.

The thatched roofs of the village begin to emit smoke at four in the morning, when the women rise to prepare the *nixtamal* and tortillas for their men, who very early make their way to the fields they have worked since the time of their earliest ancestors.

The women remain behind to weave their meager dreams of subsistence on their looms, and after nightfall they lie on their mats to ruminate in Mayan about their poverty and plan their yearly journeys to work as migrants on the coastal plantations.

That is how life has been and still goes on in this community, whose only hope is the *milpas* or cornfields they are able to scratch out of the rocky hillsides.

In the ten years since I'd arrived in the village as schoolmaster, time in the village had flown by, as the children I had the first years in my classroom grew into youths who sought marriage and made dates by the well, where the young women in their lovely native dress go to fetch water in their clay jars.

Very few of the villagers finish their sixth grade of schooling, as the great majority abandon classes after their third or fourth grades – not because they do not like schoolwork but because they must accompany their parents on their migration to the distant coastal plant-ations. This is the community's way of life. The native peoples know how to live in peace and harmony, which normally is only broken during the elections.

One such occasion was a Friday in February 1978, when several politicians arrived in the village, rabble rousing and pretending concern for the villagers' most urgent needs, beginning with the roads, which were in miserable condition. The leader of the delegation spoke his pledge in a booming voice:

"WHEN WE GAIN THE PRESIDENCY, SAN JOSE, TZALALA WILL HAVE ITS HIGHWAY, AND AS A GUARANTEE OF THIS YOU ARE TO MAKE AN X OVER THE SYMBOL OF OUR PARTY."

The villagers went to the voting booth with the hope that with their ballots they would win the promised assistance in completing the road they themselves had begun some months back with pickaxes, shovels and hoes.

After the voting, the politicians who gained good posts in the government rapidly forgot their promises.

Three years later the politicians insisted the project would be completed before long if the villagers voted again for their official candidate in the next election, so the new government could carry out the offers the previous one did not.

The community gave up expecting any results from politicians.

But what most worried the community was the formation of "civil patrols" in July of 1982.

One Sunday the military commander summoned all the head men of the surrounding villages, and there he set forth his intention to form the so-called civil defense patrols.

The entire community protested this unexpected measure, insisting they had no desire to bear arms, as this was the army's function.

The commander grew angry and declared that everyone in the village had to unite and defend

12

themselves against subversion. The people responded that they preferred to organize a labor team to carry out a project of communal benefit, such as the roads that were needed in the village and its surrounding hamlets.

The commander realized he could not convince the villagers and accepted their proposal to form a work detachment.

That is how the village and its hamlets formed into separate work groups. Once they were formed, however, the commander again summoned the heads of each group and advised them that since they were already organized into civilian detachments, they would have to go on military patrol. Those who protested this deceit by the commander were threatened with prison and were told that to oppose these measures was to be an enemy of the government.

That is how all these communities became subject to the will of the military and liable to sanctions or punishment if they disobeyed orders.

From that time on, civil patrols were in operation in Tzalalá, and they included youths of fourteen as well as old men of seventy. Under the constant pressure from the army, all the neighbors had to carry their clubs or garrotes in place of rifles and were under orders to attack any foreign elements that entered the community.

That is the background of the terrible events of September 9, 1982, when the civil patrol of Tzalalá mistook an army detachment dressed in olive fatigues for guerrillas.

13

THE ATTACK

Friday the 9th of September dawned bright and clear. The air was crystalline after a week of heavy rains. I rose very early that day and unhurriedly gathered a few things in the *morral* which I used because rucksacks of any color were too dangerous to carry around. Only the army was considered to have the right to use them, and their counterparts, the guerrillas, also carried them. I wrapped a week's used clothing in a plastic bag, next to a few bananas I'd bought from an Indian woman who travels from village to village.

Every Friday, when I returned to town, my children looked into my *morral* first thing to discover what presents I brought them. For that reason I always carry some sweets and something else for my wife and children, who always awaited my return near the outskirts of town.

I put away my cot and prepared my breakfast. I began eating at seven and by seven-fifteen I set out for the schoolhouse to begin the day's teaching. Friday has always been a happy day for me, full of the anticipation of reuniting with my family in the town, several kilometers from the village.

After our morning hygiene exercises and a quick benediction I began classes as usual. For the past several days I'd been helping the upper grades prepare some observances for Independence Day ceremonies, to be celebrated the following week. Manuelito, the most mischievous boy in the class, asked me to sing the ditty of the "Indito" or little Indian, which goes like this:

A little Indian I saw
as he danced the trot
how well he moved his feet

15

touching his own heart.
I asked, How do you do it?
Do tell me please
And he said, you just dance
the same as I do.

I realized the song was discriminatory because the questioner uses the familiar "vos" (in a vulgar sense) and the little Indian replies in a respectful USTED. For the rural child all songs taught in school are equally discriminatory, or at least alienating, because their true intention is to condition them to the requirements of the *patrón* or boss, and thereby to perpetuate the Indian's inferior status.

Manuelito insisted on singing the song, so I corrected the usages to make them the same. In the middle of our exercise the head of the civil patrol of the village burst in out of breath and gave the alarm at the top of his voice:

"The guerrillas are approaching the village. Everyone get ready!"

While he continued to shout, another member of the patrol began to ring the bell of the chapel, which signalled imminent danger.

Out of curiosity I stepped to the door and saw the villagers, or rather the first company of the civil patrol, take up their clubs, stones, slingshots and machetes and run to the aid of the front lines which guarded the entrance to the village.

The mobilization was carried out rapidly to the uninterrupted tolling of the bronze bell of the Catholic chapel.

I consulted my watch and saw it was eleven in the morning. At almost the same instant I heard the first shot fired. Behind it came a volley of machinegun fire. The peaceful community broke into confusion. The women wept and prayed to God to protect their husbands

16

and older sons who had been forced to join the civil patrol.

I ordered the students to stretch out on the floor and barred the door and windows with old broomsticks. The invaders had encircled the village and the hills echoed the furious explosions of grenades and the sputter of bullets that whistled past the corrugated tin roof of the schoolhouse.

"Don't make a sound," I ordered my children. Some began to weep and others trembled with fear. Their fathers were in the midst of that gunfire, armed only with sticks, stones and slingshots and the children were fully aware of the danger they were in.

"Pray – pray for your fathers and don't raise your heads – " I insisted. It was twelve noon and the thunderous blasts of the rifles and submachineguns continued without a pause. From time to time we heard the voice of a patrol leader who shouted in Mayan: "Keep on, *compañeros*, don't be afraid of the sons of bitches. They'll soon run out of ammunition . . . Attack!"

The voice of the patrol leader was heard on the eastern side of the schoolhouse, toward the windows. Flattened against the wall I peered under the slits of the window to locate the patrols or the attackers, but my vision was blocked and I could not see beyond a few meters. I squinted to look in all directions but could see nothing. The coffee arbor and the trees back of the school impeded my vision.

My pupils were growing restless and stretched to exercise their limbs, but I forbade them to move.

"Flatten yourselves against the floor," I ordered again as the blasts of the machineguns came closer and closer. The students obeyed and remained quiet under their desks, and I threw myself down on the floor beside them.

Immediately afterward I heard footsteps in the school patio, coming toward the door. It was a woman who began to shout for her son.

17

"Pascual, Pascualito my son, where are you? Pascual my son, come home with me."

I approached the barred door and shouted at the woman, "Your son is safe here, return to your home please and look after your other children without endangering yourself."

The woman grew angry and shouted at me: "If something happens to my son I will hold you responsible."

I paid no heed to the woman and told her son Pascual to lie down on the floor – his mother's cries had made him rise to his feet and expose himself to gunfire.

Another hour went by. It was one in the afternoon and the gunblasts were closer and louder. I began to suspect that the patrol members may have committed a grave mistake. After the mother returned to her home, I once again heard running steps in the patio. I peered through the keyhole and saw several older men running toward their homes. They too were reluctant members of the civil patrol. A military officer had forced them to join and had threatened to kill them if they refused. This officer was the same lieutenant who ordered the execution of two villagers apprehended by the patrol and who warned that anyone who refused to join the civil patrol would be considered an enemy of the government. On August 30th, exactly ten days before, the patrol had been forced to club the two men to death. The lieutenant's voice was still fresh in the minds of the villagers: "You must all look after yourselves and stop being sissies. Don't let the communist bandits into your village. Do you understand me?"

"Yes, Commander," the neighbors had shouted in unison.

"We shall see now if it's true. Kill these two motherfuckers that you yourselves apprehended."

"No," the villagers replied. "We are not accustomed to killing."

18

"Well, then, you will now become accustomed to it. Do it at once, or I will do it for you."

On August 30th the villagers had carried out their first execution.

It should not surprise anyone that even the old men and adolescents joined the patrol to escape the lieutenant's grave threats.

The old men I saw running away were in charge of guarding the school and fled for their lives when the gunfire got too close. The school and the chapel are located in the village plaza, and between them is a basketball court with an earthen floor.

I looked at my watch and saw it was 2 p.m. I felt sorry for the children stretched out on the floor. They were praying because it was all that they could do.

Fifteen minutes passed, and I was startled to hear the frantic ringing of the bell in the chapel of the village's patron saint, directly across from the school.

I peered through the keyhole once again and felt a shiver on seeing a man in olive green leading twelve patrol members with their hands tied behind them. Two other men similarly dressed pointed rifles at them. I recognized at once that the rifles they bore were Galils, of Israeli manufacture. I knew these rifles by name because the military detachment had used them in my hometown to cut down innocent people who were accused of being guerrillas.

Although the bell rang, no one approached the chapel. On other occasions the ringing of the bell would bring all the men of the village to the plaza, carrying clubs in their callused hands, and stones in their pouches for their rubber slingshots. As no one heeded the bell, the civil defender who rang it was ordered by the armed man to call at the top of his lungs and summon the villagers to gather in the school patio.

The defender filled his lungs and shouted in his own language to the villagers:

"Come close, brothers, don't be afraid. It is the army that is among us. Come quickly."

The women who had hidden in neighbors' homes when the shooting began were the first to approach. They were anxious to see if their husbands or sons were among the bound captives.

The hail of gunfire had finally ceased, and I instructed my students to rise from the floor. They sat on their desks while I opened the door and went out to the corridor to find out what was happening.

Doña Elena, who was waiting for me, approached as I left the school and began to plead with me. "I beg of you, inquire about my husband so they will release him; I don't speak Spanish and I'm afraid to speak with them."

When I saw her crying, I too felt a desire to weep, but I did not allow my tears to flow. I girded myself up and slowly approached the armed men who held the patrol members captive. I greeted them cordially and identified myself as the village schoolmaster.

The sergeant who led the captives responded in poor Spanish. By his torturous manner of speaking I deduced he was also an Indian, a native of Sololá or Totonicapán.

With an expression smeared with rage he stared at me and replied:

"Well, look here you, these bastards attacked us. We're army men and I think all these people are guerrillas."

I confirmed at first sight that they were indeed soldiers. I had begun to suspect as much when I heard the sound of their weapons. It was the same coughing noise of Galil rifles I remembered hearing when they massacred two communities on the northern trunk road, not far from the village of Tzalalá. It was the same familiar gunblasts heard when they carry out their counter-insurgency operations and sow panic in the communities they invade.

I again attempted to reason with the man, although I was aware that I was playing with fire.

"Gentlemen, these men you have bound with ropes belong to the civil patrol. They have strict orders to finish off any guerrillas that show themselves here, and that is what they mistook you for."

"Then why didn't they take notice of our rifles?"

"No doubt they failed to take notice of them, but their worst error was over the olive green uniforms you are wearing. The patrol is more familiar with the speckled camouflage fatigues commonly worn by the army."

"Wait for the lieutenant, and he will decide what to do with all of you." Saying this, the man turned his back on me.

I returned to the school and ordered my students to head directly for their homes. More soldiers leading other bound captives were arriving. Some of the patrol members were bleeding; the rest were sweating and disoriented.

When I dismissed the class and told them to go home, each of them fled like a deer out the door and raced to find his parents.

I shut the door of the school and once again I approached the civil defenders, as their women continued to weep. I felt pity for all of them, but there was very little to be done under the circumstances.

More members of the patrol arrived with their uniformed captors. They looked as if they had fled from an insane asylum. Some had broken arms from the bullets, and others had their ribs crushed from the blows of rifle butts and repeated falls. The defenders suffered in silence, without letting go the clubs they clutched in trembling hands, while the soldiers spat out curses as they shoved and kicked the villagers and rounded them all up in the patio.

WHITE FLAGS AND RESCUE

The people gathered slowly and fearfully. "Come forward without fear; these are soldiers, they are friends," the chief civil defender shouted. A poor peasant woman named Malcal approached me, saying, "Oh, schoolmaster, my child is dead. They have killed little Sebastián!"

Sebastián was a boy of fourteen who was enrolled in the sixth grade but had stopped attending classes because he had to accompany his parents to the fields. Since he stopped attending school, he had been forced to take part in the civil patrol.

It is painful to see a mother weep in agony for her dead son. This was the first death we had news of since the army began its attack on the civil patrol. Sticks are no match for the Galil rifles, and after four hours of intense combat the *kaibiles* had almost certainly emptied their cartridges on other defenseless patrol members.

At that moment I thought of leaving that devastated place, but I soon reconsidered. After ten years of teaching in that village, I thought it would be cowardice to abandon this community that was now suffering so horribly.

Another village woman approached me and pointed toward the ridge below. "Down there they have tied up many more men, and it looks as if they plan to execute them. Please find someone to help them."

"I will see what I can do," I said, and walked up to the sergeant, a dark-skinned veteran or "rehooked one," one of the soulless, unscrupulous former foot-soldiers that President Ríos Montt recruited and sent to the Indian villages during the "Offensive against Subversion."

I said to the man, "I would like to go below and speak for the men they are holding captive, and I would like a soldier to accompany me, please."

The man made a gesture of disgust but finally consented. A soldier accompanied me as I headed toward the place the woman had pointed to, about a hundred yards from the village center.

As a sign of my peaceful intention, I snatched a white flag that fluttered from the roof of a thatched hut. The white flags flew from all the huts and homes of the villages and towns in the Department of Huehuetenango, by order of the Commander of the local military detachment. The officer had announced that all those who neglected to put up the white flags would have their homes bombed by the helicopters, just as they had previously bombed the Indian community of *Coyá*.

I walked on with that little flag in my hands, and I don't know how I found the courage to try to save these endangered people. At a distance of several yards I saw the civil defenders bound together with a thick rope. They were guarded by several mean-faced soldiers.

I approached unhesitantly. One of them looked furious as he came to meet me with his rifle butt ready.

I did not give him the chance to hit me. From afar I greeted him with courtesy and brandished my white flag.

"Step forward – what do you want?"

"I wish to speak with the commanding officer."

"He's over there, take care not to upset him."

I walked toward the commander, who was seated on the threshold of a little adobe house. His shirt was unbuttoned. His bulky stomach glistened with sweat and grease.

When he saw me, he set aside some yellowed documents he was looking at and stared at me.

I recognized him as a lieutenant who during the past month had been commander of my town, but I could not recall his name. Without his asking me, I approached

24

him and leaned the white flag against the wall of the house.

"Good afternoon, my lieutenant," I said respectfully.

He turned his thick face toward me and studied me from head to foot. He was fat and short, and had a dark complexion, like the rest of his men. They were all low-ranking career soldiers.

"What do you want, you – " he snapped.

"I am the schoolmaster in this village and have come to let you know that the people you're holding captive are members of the civil patrol. By accident they mistook you for guerrillas."

"Don't come to me with those stories. These sons of bitches are guerrillas. That's why they attacked us, and I am going to execute every damn one of them."

I went on, unperturbed, "Up there by the chapel the rest of the men are waiting to clear up the situation for you."

"With me you have nothing to clear up. Everything is already clear. They've wounded one of my soldiers, and all of you will have to pay for it. What more do you want to know?"

"I beseech my lieutenant to forgive these people. All the men are members of the patrol and guard the village day and night, as you have verified for yourself. What a pity they mistook you, because of your olive green uniforms."

The commander made no reply, but went on inspecting the boxes and chests of the house. "This radio interests me. Take it along," he called out.

All the soldiers who had scattered throughout the village returned with radios and tape recorders and other objects of value they found in the houses. Clearly they had planned to sack the community, as they carried long cloth bags instead of their usual rucksacks, and they stuffed them with their spoils.

25

The captives were sitting in the middle of the road, their heads exposed to the blazing sun since they had lost their hats during the combat.

After the commanding officer was done inspecting the boxes and chests the soldiers brought him, he stood with an air of boredom and glared at me. "All right, so the people are all gathered up there, is that right?"

"Yes, they have gathered and await your arrival," I told him.

The commander buttoned his green shirt, checked the cartridge clip on his Galil and ordered his soldiers to call the others who were still sacking the more distant houses.

When they gathered in front of him the commander scolded them:

"What happened to you, you shitheads? Why didn't you obey my orders and encircle the area as I told you?"

"It's just that the guerrillas were firing at us with too much insistence, Lieutenant sir, that is why we took the other way."

"And what fucking right do you have to follow your own orders? For myself, I dragged myself to the place where these guerrillas were firing their .30 caliber; and you should have seen the bullets fly over my head, but I kept going. And you turds might as well have gone to hell. Cowards."

"No, commander sir, we didn't flee. We faced up to these cocksuckers who were shooting at us from left and right."

I laughed within me to hear them brag. The ".30 caliber" they mentioned were the stones the patrol had flung at them. The soldiers had fired at one another when they broke rank in disarray to surround the supposed guerrillas.

Only one man in the civil patrol carried an old rusty rifle the army had authorized him to use. He was a poor *campesino* inclined to do battle with the guerrillas. He had shot at the army and wounded one of them. As you seek, so shall you find, said a drunkard in prison, and that is apparently what happened to the fellow, who never had a chance to reload his rifle when a hail of bullets splintered his skull. I found this out later, for I did not witness how they gathered the corpses that night.

That single bullet had made the army quake, scattering them in all directions, and that is why the commander scolded the soldiers for disobeying his orders. After the dressing down, he placed them in single file behind the captives and ordered me to walk ahead with the white flag in my hand.

We had not gone far when a young woman raced toward us, pursued by a soldier who clutched at her dress. She was pregnant, but that made no difference to the soldier, who wanted to rape her. When she saw me at the head of the captives, she stopped to ask me for help in her native language, which the soldiers did not understand. She trembled with fear but still fought back bravely with nails and teeth against the warped intentions of the soldier.

The commander caught on and rebuked the soldier, who brazenly protested he was after her only because she was concealing something. The officer laughed aloud and told us to keep marching.

I went ahead with my little plastic flag, and the captives followed behind me, their hands tied with a single rope.

We could not walk fast because one of the bound captives was an old man whose right foot was wounded, and he left bloody prints on the ground with each step. The commander became impatient and shouted at the old man in a fury:

"Hurry up you old fucker. That's what you get for playing at guerrillas."

The old man replied in the Spanish he had learned as a soldier in the time of Jorge Ubico:

27

"Go easy on me, chief, I am old already and know something about the army. The only reason I'm here is because they forced me to join the patrol. At my age I should be relaxing under the shade of my little hut."

The commander cut him off and shoved the old man so he fell on the ground, bringing down the others who were bound with the same rope.

"You old turd, if you open your mouth again I'll fill you full of lead right here. An old bastard like you has no right to live."

"Do with me what you please, brother, since even a woman with a rifle in hand could do the same."

The old man paid for his retort with a fist in the face that loosened his few remaining teeth. I didn't dare say anything because I saw the soldiers were furious and there was no sense in suffering blows for nothing.

We finally reached the basketball court in front of the school, where the villagers were gathered, while nearly all the patrol members were tied to the oaken posts that held up the hoops. I planted the white flag at the school entrance and sat down sorrowfully to see what would happen next.

I WATCHED MY SON DIE

Before going down to rescue the captives I had learned of the death of one patrol member: the boy of fourteen who had been in my class at the start of the year. When I returned to the village center the wailing and weeping of the women had grown louder. As the defenders joined the gathering, each gave his account of the *compañeros* that had fallen in combat.

It was now two-thirty, and the day had begun to cloud over. The bullet-riddled bodies of the dead civil defenders remained where they had fallen. No one, not even the widows, dared to leave the group to weep over the bodies of their husbands.

The only corpse with a roof over it was that of the fourteen-year-old son of the woman who had spoken to me, Doña Malcal.

"I saw it all," she told me. "My son had just arrived with a bundle of firewood when the shooting broke out. He dropped the load without untying it and ran down the hill where we live to look for his father.

"No, Sebastián, stay here and hide!" I said to him, but he would not heed me. He kept on running down the hill while the bullets whistled and struck the adobe wall of our house. He was my only son, and because I knew the risk he was taking, I went after him. I could hardly run as I was carrying my small daughter at my hip, and by the time I got below, my son was crouched behind some large rocks with another defender I was unable to identify.

"The noise made by the firearms of the attackers was like that of firecrackers at a festival, only much louder, and it gave us a terrible fright. Even so, I ignored the bullets that flew past and knelt down where my son was. I pulled at his shirt and shouted so he could hear me. 'Let's go home, I'm afraid of your being here. Come, my son,

29

let's go home.' He turned abruptly and said, 'Mother, why have you followed me? Don't you see you're running a risk for yourself and the little one? Go on home and hide, and don't worry about me.'

"Since I could not persuade my son, I crouched low and ran back. Before I reached the door of our hut I heard a scream behind me and turned to see my son crumpled behind the rock. I ran down again and called out, 'Sebastián, what has happened my son?' He lifted his face toward me and said, 'They've hit me, Mother, but don't worry; go on back to the house before they get you too.'

"I saw at once that his face had grown pale. Blood began to cover his shirt, and the color had started to fade from his eyes.

"'Oh my son, Sebastiáncito, they've wounded you!' I cried aloud, and hugged him to my breast.

"'Leave me, Mother, don't grieve over me, leave me here and go back home to protect yourself and the little one.'

"'No my son, I don't want to leave you. I want to stay here and die with you because you are my only male child.'

"Sebastián looked into my eyes and smiled. He was very white and began to lose his strength. I unbuttoned his shirt and was horrified to see the bullet hole in his back, just above the lungs. My eyes clouded and I held him to myself with all my strength. 'Does it hurt much, my son?' I asked, and he replied:

"'No, not much. I only feel something warm flowing through my body.' And he began to vomit up blood. I did not wait any longer, but shifted my daughter to the front and lifted him across my back. I ran frenziedly toward the house, with the bullets flying all around and dodged between the houses as I fled with my son up the hill.

"I pushed the door open with my foot and lay my son down on the wooden pallet. I quickly gathered up some eggs laid by the black hen and made a broth to staunch my son's wound. But with every sip he took he vomited up more blood and could not keep it down. I lifted his head onto my chest and caressed it tenderly, as I had when he was little.

"'Oh my son, you should never have left the house! Last night I had bad dreams and felt a danger for you.'

"Sebastián looked sadly into my eyes and replied with difficulty. 'Don't weep for me, one never knows what's going to happen. Don't weep, Mother, these fourteen years I 've lived with you count for something.'

"His last words were spoken slowly, torturously, and a dark shadow came over the whites of his eyes. 'Don't die my son! Please don't die . . . Oh my God!' I gathered him in my arms and kissed him again and again, bathing his pale face with my tears. Then I ran outside and began shouting from the hilltop with all my strength for my husband so he could come and see our dying son. My voice was trembling, and my calls probably did not reach very far. The gunfire had grown louder, and I saw several men withdrawing from their positions as the enemy approached. I returned inside the house and sat down next to my dying son. I began to weep aloud, until the women next door came over to see what happened.

"The first one to come was Sebastián's grandmother, and the other two were my sisters-in-law. They had not been aware of what happened to Sebastián because they had been lying motionless on the floor of their house and had not dared go out for fear of getting shot. I was grateful they arrived when I needed them most. With them there, I felt more secure and was able to grieve openly. The grandmother lifted up Sebastián in her wrinkled arms and began to weep aloud as she kissed his face.

"But my son no longer felt anything. His breathing was torturous and short. Again I tried to spoon-feed him an egg beaten with orange juice to give him strength, but it was useless because his jaw was growing rigid. I pried open his mouth with both fingers and struggled to make

31

him swallow a little of the potion. But his agonizing moans frightened me and I put the glass aside.

"It was no use, my son had to die, and I could do nothing but weep. We boarded up the door and all wept together to see my dear son dying little by little, painfully.

"His grandmother began to curse the authors of this calamity, but as a mother I did not wish to do so. I resigned myself. I realized that just as God had given me my son, so he was gathering him up. It is not that I do not love my son, but that I love him the same as all mothers love their sons. I gain nothing by cursing. I placed everything in the hands of God because I know He will mete out justice for all the good as well as the evil that is done.

"There was a loud banging on the door, and we threw ourselves down on the wooden cot where my son lay in agony.

"'Open up or I'll set fire to the house!' shouted the man who pounded on the door. This frightened my mother-in-law because if he set fire to our straw roof, the entire house would go up in a blaze, with us inside it. She rose slowly and, hunched as she was with age, she removed the bolt from the door. At that moment the man kicked the door in, and she was flung against the open fireplace.

"'Let's see how many guerrillas you are hiding here!' said the man, who wore leather army boots and carried a regulation rifle. This awakened my doubts, and I realized that he indeed was a soldier by the way he carried himself. The guerrillas had passed through the village now and then, and those who had seen them said they wear rubber boots and cause no harm to anyone. That is how I realized the invaders of our village were army soldiers – by their rough manner and the harm they were causing us.

"The man approached my dying son and began to lift him to his feet, but I threw myself on top of Sebastián to prevent the man from causing him further harm.

"'Don't touch him, he is my son and he is dying. There are no guerrillas here, only civil defenders. You forced them to form into patrols, and now you yourselves are killing them.'

"He seized me by the hair and pulled me to my feet, shouting furiously. 'These lousy motherfuckers attacked us, and I want to see the face of this bastard to make him tell me where he hid his weapon and his uniform.'

"'No, señor,' I replied, weeping bitterly. 'We are Christians here, poor peasants who know nothing of such things.'

"As I spoke, the man began to search our small hut, flinging the clothes hanging from the line onto the floor and spilling the baskets of corn and beans we kept in storage. He even grabbed the hen that was laying eggs in one corner and flung her onto the patio.

"'Well, it's you poor campesinos who get mixed up in the bullshit,' the man replied. His words made me angry, for I felt certain this villain was as poor as we are, but he acted like one of the rich. Much as I wanted to throw this up in his face, it was not the time to make accusations. My husband, who has some learning, had said, 'With the soldiers words are useless, because they are brutes, and brutes only know how to use force.'

"The man went on ransacking the house until he found the small box where I kept some silver earrings my husband had given me for a wedding present. The soldier did not ask for the key; he placed the box on the ground and splintered it with the butt of his rifle. The few objects of value we kept inside flew out of the crushed box, and the soldier dropped them in the sack he carried on his back. He even took some colored ribbons I had labored many hours to weave.

33

"'Please,' I pleaded, 'don't take my earrings,' but he stepped toward me furiously as if ready to strike me.

"'I don't want any arguments from you, you old cunt. If you open your mouth one more time, I'll split it open with one blow.'

"The soldier barefacedly continued to stuff his sack, until there was nothing left that interested him. He ordered us: 'Now you will join the other shitheads of this village out by the chapel.'

"'No *señor*, I am staying here with my dying son. I cannot leave him alone, in his condition. Please take pity on us.'

"'Leave him here to rot,' the villain replied, 'and you go on where I ordered you. Now, quickly.'

"He pushed us out of the house, and I had to leave my son behind. That is why I am here now like a ghost, while my heart remains with my son, who by now is almost certainly dead."

This is what the woman told me in Mayan language, while I watched with my own eyes the soldiers searching all the houses of the community, like hungry dogs. Small groups of women and children were marched to the chapel by their captors, and the murmurs of the assembled grew louder, as the women and children wept openly. The men remained deathly still. In the faces of each of the civil defenders I could see fear. They seemed dazed and unable to grasp their situation. Or perhaps they understood and regretted their mistakes. They had gone out determined to wipe out an unknown enemy and had met the very men who had professed to be their friends and protectors. Even the dimmer ones had occasion to reflect on their actions.

THE BLACKLIST

As soon as the soldiers and villagers had gathered next to the chapel, the commanding officer gave the order for the women and children to be taken inside.

When the women and children were inside the chapel, the soldiers stood guard as the men remained still, standing or sitting on the school steps, awaiting the next development with dazed expressions.

The lieutenant ordered the villagers to form according to the squad they belonged to, "And have in your hands your civil patrol identity card."

He then pulled out a sheet of paper from his pocket, which he unfolded with an impatient flourish. He smoothed the paper against his thigh and warned the troops to keep a sharp eye and not let anyone move from their place.

The soldiers encircled the group at once and released the safety catches of their Galils, pointing them with lizard eyes at the villagers, ready to shoot the first one to make a move.

"You will pass in front of me with your identity card in your hand," the lieutenant barked, fixing eyes brimming with malice on the villagers, to study their reactions.

The villagers understood that the lieutenant had a list in his possession, which made their situation that much more precarious. Several soldiers behind the commander prepared ropes to tie up those to be singled out. As the first defenders passed before the lieutenant, the tension steadily mounted.

In that climate, anyone can condemn to death his own neighbor with the slightest accusation or rumor. It has become conveniently easy to get rid of a person for reasons of revenge or other personal differences, simply by denouncing him to the army as a leftist sympathizer.

The fear became evident in the villagers' faces, as they marched with their cards in hand before the lieutenant and his list.

"God save us," some of them whispered. "It is easier to defend yourself from a dagger or a bullet than from a false accusation."

About ten of the patrol members had filed past when the first of them fell into the army's hands. The lieutenant read his card and matched his name to one he had on the list. He made a signal with his head, and two soldiers immediately grabbed the youth and tied him to the basketball post. They tied him fast, with his hands in back, and beat him furiously on the face and stomach.

More men filed past, and then another was pulled out of the line. "Take this one too, his name is on the list," the commander snapped, and the soldiers carted him off with the other, like devils leading the souls of the condemned to hell.

Several more of the villagers passed inspection, as the soldiers untied their ropes and shoved them in line to show their identity papers. By this time, five had been picked out, but the commander was annoyed that he had not yet found the one he was looking for. Glaring at those he had inspected he remarked: "I still don't have the son of a bitch who trained these guerrillas. They say he is a *kaibil* who only recently left the service. Do any of you know him? Where is he?"

I stepped forward to answer in the name of the others. "My commander, we don't know who that may be. Possibly he is not among us."

I said this to prevent someone from becoming an accomplice to the scoundrel who had presented the list and condemned these men to be slaughtered.

About five minutes later the ex-soldier they were looking for showed up, returning from the front lines of defense farthest from the village.

"Follow that one," the lieutenant ordered, as the young man passed us on his way to find his wife, whom he had only recently married, among the women inside the chapel.

"I didn't bring my identity card," he told his wife, who tried to leave the group of women under custody so she could fetch it from their house. But the soldiers who were sent after him did not let her go.

"Come here, you," they said, taking the young man by the arm. "The commander wants a word with you."

The ex-*kaibil*, who still wore the close-cut hair style of the special forces, walked toward the commander with a proud bearing.

He remained stiffly erect as the commander questioned him:

"What is your name?"

"Antonio."

"Your full name, turd!"

"Antonio M. López."

"Aha, so we got you, motherfucking traitor."

As he said this, the commander kicked him in the testicles and shoved his rifle butt against his face, flinging him to the ground. The other soldiers kicked him until he bled, then stood him up and tied his hands behind his back with tight knots.

The youth remained silent, with his head held high.

It was three fifteen, and the defenders who belonged to the second shift began returning from the fields. The agreement was that the two companies took turns guarding the village and working the fields, spelling one another.

The new arrivals were not allowed to return to their homes, but were forced to line up and present their credentials, the same as the others. At the head was a young man of seventeen, who unloaded his burro in the school patio and then presented his birth certificate. They checked his name against the list, and unfortunately it appeared there, so they bound him up with the others.

To speed up the inspection the soldiers gathered the identity cards in several hats and took them to the lieutenant. For some reason, he returned them to their owners without having inspected them all.

After consulting his watch the lieutenant ordered his sergeant to pick out the tallest among the listed captives and lead him inside the school.

"What for?" the sergeant asked.

"What for, you blockhead! Take him in so he can tell you some jokes."

The "jokes" meant he would be tortured until he "confessed," even if it was all lies.

They took the youth inside and barred the door. The lieutenant who sat in the patio radioed his superiors and asked for a helicopter to take out the wounded soldier. A part of his code was easily decipherable.

"Potato calling here. Combat with guerrillas in zones P . . . . and M . . . . Several captured. Over."

When he finished, he ordered the villagers to cut down the basketball posts, so the helicopter could land on the court. The neighbors ran to fetch their axes, and without having to be told twice, began chopping at the two posts.

Until recently the only entertainment in the village had been drinking the local rotgut, and so a few of us had planned the basketball court, and with the aid of several youngsters had cut down two oak trees and carved out the posts. It had not been easy to build this court because everything made in our village we did with our own hands, without any help from the authorities. Still, in the present circumstances it was too risky to defy the commander, who stood smiling with satisfaction, his

38

black Galil pointed at us as he surveyed the scene of destruction.

Several of us supported the posts so they would not crash to the ground and splinter the backboards to which the hoops had been screwed. We prevented the destruction of what had cost so much sacrifice to complete and planned to replace the posts as soon as the invaders left the village.

Until that moment I had been sitting quietly next to some friends and near the lieutenant, who paced impatiently among his soldiers, flaunting his list.

I thought of those whose names were on the list. Some of them had seen the danger coming and had hidden out somewhere a few days earlier; the incautious ones now had ropes tied around their necks. I wondered too about the cowardly villain who had anonymously presented the list. How craven to betray a neighbor in that way – far worse than killing him with weapon in hand.

At first I thought some of the captives would attempt to flee, but it did not turn out that way. They all remained silent, unmoving; only their faces expressed their confusion. Those poor young men had fallen into the hands of criminal soldiers, who acted without waiting to verify the source or the motive behind the lists they held in their hands.

The army officers know they will rise in rank in accordance with the number of unfortunates they execute. It is a sort of rivalry encouraged among these officers who behave with such cruelty and savagery and destroy entire Indian communities without remorse.

ACCUSATIONS

I remained seated under the eaves of the chapel, watching in consternation the captives who gazed vacantly at some undefined point in the horizon. Very close by, the commander scratched his buttocks with his nails, trying to loosen the trousers that pinched his overblown body.

The sergeant appeared with a soldier, holding in his hand a scrap of paper I recognized as a matchbook cover. He presented it to the commander with a show of gravity.

"What happened?" the lieutenant asked him.

"Well, he confessed."

"What did he say?"

"He gave a name. Here it is."

The sergeant handed him the matchbook cover and whispered in his ear, too softly for me to hear. The commander turned on me a fixed glare. I suspected nothing, but as he stood over me I had the sense that something bad was about to happen.

"You're the prof here, is that right?" the commander asked.

"Sí mi comandante, what can I do for you?"

My forthright reply set him aback. Without further commentary, he snapped at me: "Follow these men."

The sergeant and the soldier escorted me to my classroom, where they had taken the tall dark youth a while back so he would "tell some jokes."

They opened the door and pushed me inside, then closed it shut, leaving me entirely at their mercy.

Manuel lay face down on the floor, in a pool of blood, with his hands tied behind his back. His face looked grotesquely disfigured.

I sat down on one of the old desks of the classroom, showing neither fear nor nervousness. I knew that if I betrayed weakness I would lose any advantage I would have during the interrogation. I gathered up my strength and would not humble myself before these men, who regarded me like hungry wolves. I focussed my mind so I would not stumble over my own words or fall into the traps they were setting for me.

Six soldiers stood over me, pointing their black Galils at my head with malicious smiles on their lips. I turned aside to avoid their twisted scowls, with which they tried to intimidate me. A soldier approached from behind, ready to place a noose around my neck to choke me. I rose from my seat at once. If I allowed them to strike me at the outset without defending myself, I would lose my hard-won confidence. I stood up before he had a chance to collar me and looked into their eyes.

"*Señores*," I said in a firm voice, "I am no criminal for you to be assaulting me without reason. I ask to know what I am accused of, as I consider myself innocent."

"As innocent as the great whore," the sergeant called out. "Here is your accuser. You are a guerrilla, the same as your companion."

He addressed the tortured youth, shouting, "All right, you fucker – tell your companion what you confessed to us. Go on, wretch."

As he said this the sergeant began to kick him in the face, the head and the stomach. I almost broke down seeing the blows he gave Manuel. I've never been able to tolerate the sight of a suffering fellow being. Whenever my mother slaughters a hen for dinner or a fiesta I always turn aside so I won't have to see its neck twisted. Now that I beheld a human being tortured and bloodied, I felt a great heaviness and fear.

Despite his wretched state, Manuel turned his head toward me with difficulty and spoke with hatred, spitting out blood on the floor.

"Look brother, I heard your voice one night when two men came to threaten me, calling me a loudmouth

42

reactionary, and I am certain that you were one of them. I am sure I heard your voice."

As he finished speaking a soldier reached out one hand and punched me in the midsection, causing me to double over with pain. To avoid another blow, I sat down quickly on the old desk, as the sergeant said to me with gloating disdain:

"Now we have you and you can't get out of this one. You heard your own companion accuse you."

"That accusation has no validity," I said, with strained dignity. "Many people in this world have the same or similar voices, and this man who accused me falsely, is lying. I would never oppose the government – I am a schoolteacher and my salary is paid by the State. Let this young man tell you when he has seen me break any law. If he can accuse me of acting illegally and prove it, I am ready to pay the consequences; but if he can't, I plead with you to let me go because I assure you that I know nothing of these matters."

They began pummelling Manuel once again, shouting: "Speak up, shit-face, what else do you know about this two-bit schoolmaster?"

"I know nothing more," the beaten youth replied. "I only know that he accompanied the one who threatened me that night, and that he is a guerrilla."

I turned to Manuel and said, "Look, Manuel, don't accuse me falsely. It's better if you resign yourself. Better to die alone and without remorse than to drag others to their death. What will you gain by killing me?"

He replied with great effort, "Well, I want them to kill you, too. We can die together."

Manuel had been an easy-going sort, with a cheerful disposition. When we met in the streets he always greeted me, and we played soccer together now and then. He had the reputation in the village of being a loudmouth, which is why he may have been threatened by one of the men he mistook me for.

43

Disregarding his words, I entreated with him softly, while I prayed inside me for him to take back his accusation. And so that the soldiers would ask me no more questions, I hastily pointed out:

"You see, *señores*, he can prove nothing against me. And as a Christian, I know perfectly well it does no good to kill one another."

The sergeant stepped toward me in a rage. "Look, little schoolmaster son of *la chingada*, don't you come off giving us any orders." And he struck me in the face with the knotted rope. But I remained unmoved, looking him directly in the eyes.

One of the soldiers who sat at a corner table got up and tried to calm down his fellows. "That's enough, boys. Stop behaving like such shits."

The sergeant dismissed him with a withering look and stood on top of Manuel, who remained face down on the floor, and began jumping up and down, coming down hard on his lungs and chest. Not satisfied with this, he kicked him once more on the left cheek until more blood flowed from his nose and mouth. The sergeant shouted like one demented:

"There will be no pity for these motherfuckers. They deserve to be kicked to death like this. Did you hear me, turd?" He went on taunting Manuel. "Where are your companions? And what else do you know about this little schoolmaster?"

Manuel did not utter another word, but could only whimper each time the sergeant kicked him savagely in the side.

The commander walked in just then, and ordered the sergeant to take us out and place us with the other captives. They quickly picked up the bloodied Manuel, who could hardly stand, and pushed him out the door. I did not wait but walked directly behind the commander.

It was like emerging from a tunnel. I looked up with gratitude at the open sky, but my spirits fell on hearing

44

the screams of the women who were shut up inside the chapel.

While I was being interrogated in the school, the lieutenant had ordered the beating of the other captives, and I saw they all had cracked lips and teeth stained with blood.

The commander kept on shouting and insisting they point out their companions, whose names did not appear on the list. The younger ones all kept quiet, even as they were beaten and screamed at. Their silence provoked the fury of the commander, who began firing his rifle crazily into the air.

The screams of the women in the chapel grew louder. Several of them, particularly the mothers of the captives, tried to get outside, but the guards threatened to crack their skulls open.

The commander kept up his inquisitorial questioning, but no one said a word. It was clear they did not know anything.

"Whichever of you speaks up will be spared," the commander said, and one of the bound captives opened his mouth to speak. They grabbed him by the hair and lifted him to his feet.

"Finally, we have one willing to talk. Speak up, wretch," the commander roared furiously. "Who are your accomplices?"

The dazed man looked around him, as if in a trance. He looked over the entire group, not knowing where to rest his eyes. Finally, he pointed somebody out. "That one – " he said, jabbing his finger at one of the civil defenders who still held his polished *garrote* in one hand. The defender began to shake, as two soldiers pulled him out of the group.

"No *señores*, I'm not anything," the man blubbered. "You are mistaken – "

His neighbors stepped forward to defend him.

45

"*No, señor comandante.* This man is one of the civil defenders who most incites us to battle the guerrillas. And he is one of the richest men in the community."

The lieutenant released the defender, who returned to his place looking white as a sheet.

I had not given much thought to my own situation until then. Only when they released the defender did I become aware that I had a rope around my neck. I stood in the center of the plaza like a thief or a murderer, exposed to the stares of the entire community, whose intentions toward me at the moment I could not tell. I felt like one condemned.

When one of the villagers I considered a friend walked past me, I addressed him in a soft voice. "Look, friend, do me the favor of speaking to the headman, so they will intercede for me. Let them say they know me as the schoolmaster of the village, and they have not seen me engage in any subversive activities."

But this friend stepped backward as if it were the very devil speaking to him. All he said was, "I am afraid."

A while later one of the headmen who had spoken up for the defender came near, and I signalled to him to aid me in the same way, but he only replied with hand signals, opening his palm as though to say, "Wait."

I knew that answer was equivalent to a "No," and so I decided to remain quiet. I had no other recourse but to gaze up at the sky and go on praying for my captive friends, for my family and for myself.

It was now four in the afternoon. Every Friday by this time I would be with my family, playing with my children. But now I had fallen into the hands of these tyrants, and I feared I would never see my children again.

I did not want anyone to see my tears, and turned my face up toward the sky, which had clouded over. I called to mind my brother, who had been killed by the *kaibiles* – he was the first innocent to have been cut down in my town by the machinegun bursts of the special army units.

The idea took hold in my head that he was sitting in the clouds and looking down at me with a reassuring smile. I thought also about my parents, and of the other brothers who were some distance away, unaware of what had befallen me.

I turned my back to the plaza and could not recognize the faces of my acquaintances. My vision was blurred by the tears that had sprung from my eyes; I looked at everyone as though in a dream. Wherever I looked, the men crouched and avoided my eyes, turning to one side.

THE HELICOPTER

About half an hour after the commander had radioed, we heard the distant sound of the helicopter. All the defenders turned toward the source of the droning sound, beyond the hills. As the noise grew louder, panic spread among the neighbors, and then the helicopter appeared, all at once above the summit of the nearest hill. It was one of the new models, blue and white and heavily armored. It circled the village several times before it began its descent.

The lieutenant gave the order to clear the basketball court whose posts had already been removed. The "whirlybird," as the children of our region called it, descended slowly, veering carefully to avoid the corrugated tin roofs of the chapel and the school. Everyone covered their mouths to keep from breathing in the dust and leaves picked up by the propellers, which stirred up a gale that sucked out our breath.

The helicopter could not land in the cleared basketball court so it rose again, reversing its pattern of descent.

The consternation was immense, particularly among the women who set up a din in the chapel which allowed some of them to slip out to the patio to look for their men.

The commander approached me and said, "You seem to know a good deal. You'll get on the helicopter together with the ex-*kaibil*, trainer of guerrillas, so you can be dealt with by the specialists at the base."

The helicopter had landed in the soccer field, about 400 meters from the village center. They tied me more securely, and the sergeant pulled me by the rope tied to my neck so I had to run behind him.

Antonio, the other captive, also had to jog along as they kicked him and shoved him toward the helicopter, which was kicking up a whirlwind of dust and dry grass from the neglected soccer field.

"You'd better walk on in front of me, you shit-face," the sergeant said in his primitive Spanish, acquired without schooling. He tugged hard at the end of the rope, causing me to trip and fall. I went on, half running and stumbling, down the slope toward the helicopter, whose propellers continued to whip the air and lift debris into the sky.

As we crossed a stream about thirty meters from the field, the commander went ahead to speak with the two officers who had come in the helicopter. The wind raised by the propellers lashed at my face, and I feared the blades would slice off my head. Antonio also remained immobile, blinking repeatedly to prevent the dust from stinging his eyes.

I felt a dreadful depression at that moment and turned for a last look at the hillsides behind the village, convinced that I would never see them again. Against the clouded sky, four or five swallows dipped and darted, announcing rain.

The commander had to shout into the officers' ears to be heard above the deafening racket of the helicopter. When he was finished, the lieutenant stepped aside and ordered me to climb into the craft, at the same time that the soldier wounded by the civil patrol was taken aboard on the other side. I lowered my head and placed a foot inside. The floor of the helicopter was covered with Galil rifles, some hand grenades and several boxes of ammunition. When one of the officers became aware of my presence, he shouted:

"Get him out, get him out, tie him up hand and foot. Can't you see there are guns in here?"

The sergeant who was still holding me, gave a hard tug at the rope and I fell to the ground on my back. I got up immediately to deny them the opportunity to strike me. Just as I stood up, the doors of the helicopter closed and it lifted at once, taking only the wounded soldier. The lieutenant cursed at the sky as the helicopter took off without us. He flung his weapon to the ground and grabbed the soldier with the radio on his back.

"Come back, come back, take the two captives!" he shouted furiously, spitting into the tiny microphone of the radio transmitter.

His shouts filled me with despair, but they melted into the air as the helicopter continued its flight to Huehuetenango.

When the helicopter finally disappeared behind the hill, I felt a twinge of relief in my chest. I still was not free, but at least I was on home soil. If they killed me, it was far better for my body to lie on my native soil, where I had been raised since childhood, than to be flung from on high into a river, a mountain slope or the crater of a volcano.

The sergeant who had bound me tight, undid the rope around my neck. I had been tied back to back with Antonio, lashed into a single bundle that would have been easier to dispose of.

It seemed a miracle to me that we had not been flown away, and I thanked the Virgin inwardly for Her favors.

"Let's get back up!" the commander shouted, and we got back on the trail to the village, as I became aware for the first time of the depredations of the soldiers, who had burned the straw and adobe huts of the poorest families.

"Burn that other one," the commander ordered, and three soldiers poured gasoline over the posts of an adobe hut and set it ablaze. One by one they destroyed several houses in the community.

51

We walked on, followed by the lieutenant, who kept on spitting out curses and kicking loose stones along the trail.

I stopped to catch my breath when we reached the small bridge that fords the stream just before the climb back to the village center. I decided to try to speak with the commander once more, and as he approached from behind, I said:

"*Mi comandante*, I beseech you to understand my situation. I know nothing of what I am accused of."

"Shut up, you piece of shit – " the sergeant cut me off.

"I'm not speaking to you, I was addressing the commander," I said in a firm voice. The commander had heard me, and replied, "You have nothing to ask of me. If I wanted to, I could shoot you on the spot – but I consider it more important to take you to Huehue to the G-2 agents."

I had no choice but to stay silent. Ahead of me walked Antonio, with his hands bound tight and a loaded rucksack on his back. Despite the weight, and the rope chafing at his neck, he walked rigidly erect, refusing to bend for anyone. When they struck him, he didn't say a word.

As we approached the patio where everyone was gathered, the men stretched their necks out for a look at us – they thought the helicopter had taken us away. But fate decreed that we look once again on the frightened faces of the villagers. Among them, almost certainly, was the villain who had brazenly submitted the anonymous list to the army, sentencing his brothers to death.

I looked around me and spat on the ground. I felt a terrible thirst and hoped someone would bring me water to drink. Thirst was the only thing I felt. Although I had not eaten lunch, I had not the slightest desire for food.

In the midst of the confusion in the patio, I once again heard the sound of a helicopter. At first it sounded like the grinder of our *nixtamales*, but I soon distinguished the peculiar drone of the dreaded whirlybird.

"This time you won't get off," the commander taunted me. "The helicopter is coming back."

Once more the sergeant took the end of the rope and ordered me to move quickly toward the helicopter, which was circling above the field.

I felt the heaviness return. Once again my wife and children filled my thoughts:

'My children, I will not see you again. How I longed to see you grow up, and always be at your side; but now my hopes are vanishing. I will not know what becomes of you. Goodbye, my children.'

"Let's go, shit-face," the sergeant yelled.

Without heeding him, I walked at my own pace. We crossed the small bridge that fords the stream in the outskirts of the village, and passed once more the burnt huts, whose straw roofs had turned to ashes.

From afar I saw the helicopter hover above the soccer field, with its motor roaring and its propeller blades slicing the air with invisible strokes.

"Hurry up, you piece of shit!" the sergeant shouted, as he dragged me like an animal to slaughter, a step behind the commander, who leaped over the stream that skirts the sports field.

At that moment the sound of the helicopter changed in pitch, and before I could ford the stream, the craft lifted and headed west, in the direction of the Mexican border.

The commander let loose a curse. Again he grabbed hold of the soldier carrying the radio transmitter on his back, and screamed into it, in repeated bursts: "Come back. Turn around and pick up the captives."

But the pilot made no response, and the helicopter kept going until it vanished in the horizon.

The first time I approached the helicopter I had noticed that the officers occupying it belonged to the so-called elite or privileged officer class – bourgeois army men who differed in every way from the commander and his foot soldiers; these last were all of dark complexion and ill-educated – alienated Indians who like rabid dogs had been sent by their ranking officers to the villages to finish off their own people.

I felt a wave of relief on realizing that danger once again seemed to recede. The first time, I had set foot inside the helicopter before I was pushed away, and this time I did not even get as far as the soccer field. I thanked God once again that I had been given a few added moments of life.

On this second scramble to chase after the helicopter, Antonio was no longer beside me. He had remained behind with the others in the school patio.

The commander turned to me angrily. "Well, little schoolmaster, now it looks like you've remained in our hands. Let's go back up to join your companions. And you – birdshit soldiers – let's see you stretch a leg and fetch that box of ammunition left by the helicopter. Don't fall asleep on me, fuckfaces, or I'll knock your wind out with a single blow."

He went on haranguing the soldiers, who reacted like automatons. Two of them hurried to follow orders and lifted the metal box containing the ammunition.

We then climbed back up toward the village center. I looked at my watch. It was 4:30. I had not even noticed it was late afternoon.

THE EXECUTION

Once again we came to the large patio that separated the school from the chapel, where the villagers all stood silent, with heads lowered. The only voices to be heard were those of the soldiers, as they bullied and shoved people about.

I was bothered by the knotted rope around my neck and stuck my fingers repeatedly under the noose to prevent it from choking me. My dignity as a schoolmaster, I said to myself. These bastards are making a display of me, as if I were an assassin, a thief or a common criminal. I spat my darkest unspoken thoughts on the ground. What President Lucas García had left undone during his brutal term in office was now being completed by his successor Efraín Ríos Montt. In all my thirty years I had not known darker days than the present ones.

The last time I had been to the provincial capital of Huehuetenango, the only place where you can keep abreast of national and international developments, I had read in a newspaper the astute Ríos Montt's proclamations: "I belong to a religious congregation in which we give thanks to God, keep faith with the word of God, and practice the word of God."

I smiled inwardly. What cynicism. What a shameless liar. I had never thought the coup that overthrew Lucas García would in any way improve conditions in the country. So long as the same army officers who weave and manipulate the political offal remain in power, the situation would remain unchanged, because whatever puppet they install in the presidency would be incapable of controlling the abuses of his military chiefs, who are the real bosses of the government and of the country.

"All of you, form a semicircle to witness the execution of these filthy guerrillas." The villagers responded sluggishly to the commander's order until they formed a large semicircle. About four hundred civil defenders gathered with their heads lowered, polished clubs still clutched in their hands, ready to witness another feat of the military commander, who was certain to be promoted in rank for killing so many "guerrillas."

Two more villagers appeared with bales of corn on their back, poor farmers returning from their milpas. When their names turned up on the list, they were immediately set upon by the soldiers and placed with the other captives. They were not given time to tie their burros to the posts outside the school or to remove the ragged cloth they used for a saddle, which betrayed their humble peasant origins. For the commander, this alone would have been proof enough of their complicity, for in his eyes, to be a *campesino*, to be poor, was to be a guerrilla.

"Tie those cowards to the posts," yelled the commander. Soldiers were quick to obey his orders. They seized the first six youths and bound them to the pillars of the unpainted adobe municipal building, in full view of the villagers. Once again the hoarse and odious voice of the commander rose above the silent witnesses – men, women and children.

"*Señores*, we are now going to demonstrate to you that we do not fear the guerrillas. Open your eyes wide, all of you, so you can see how we deal with the enemies of our government. We have been given orders to kill, and that is what we intend to do. So keep in mind that if there are any more guerrillas among you, like these mother-fuckers, we will dispatch them in the same way."

The villagers lowered their eyes. None of them wanted to see or hear anything more from this monster who had plunged the entire community into mourning.

56

The five condemned men turned to one another, uncomprehending. They set their eyes above the heads of the *kaibiles* who were lining up to discharge their weapons into their hearts. No one spoke. The hapless captives gazed toward the horizon, as though to bid farewell to the hills that had nurtured them. The *campesino* feels he is a part of nature. He spends all his life bound to it like a bud or an unseverable and timeless offshoot.

I have become familiar with what a man thinks about in the moments before his death. Nothing! At that instant the mind clouds, the eyes grow vague and heavy and the body lightens. But then, all at once like electric charges the most marvelous and forgotten landscapes return to his mind's eye. Afterward come his wife and children, his parents, and finally, the infinite. This is the last frame the mind projects in one's final moments of existence.

Antonio, the ex-military, was bound to one of the pillars to await the execution order. He held to his grave and silent demeanor, as his wife and parents wept aloud. The only one unaware of what was about to befall him was his eighteen-month-old daughter, who laughed and played with her mother's earrings.

The women who had taken refuge could no longer withstand their confinement and rushed outside, screaming, although a few chose to remain in the chapel and pray aloud to the Holy Father to summon his justice and prevent the spilling of innocent blood in these Indian fields. Meanwhile, the commander had lined up the firing squad, and raised his voice:

"RRReady . . . !"

The parents and relatives of the condemned attempted to throw themselves on their sons to shield their bodies, but they were savagely repelled with rifle butts by the foot soldiers, who openly bragged of their

57

disdain for the parents and of their scathing contempt for their "fucking" children.

As the commander prepared to give the fatal order, the condemned turned instinctively for a last look at their loved ones. Their hands were tied behind their back so they could give vent to their feelings only with strained smiles and bitter tears.

"FIRE . . . !" The cavernous voice of the commander rang out, and the Galils exploded with thunderous fury.

The women raised a deafening howl. Dazed with grief, they tried to fling themselves on the bullet-riddled bodies of their beloved ones, but once again the *kaibiles* forced them to draw back by threatening to shoot them point blank.

The victims slumped and hung from the pillars as the warm, copious blood drenched their shirts.

"Stay clear – keep back or I'll shoot all of you – " the commander shouted. "There's no reason to weep for these cowards!"

His threats stilled the clamor of the villagers until José, one of the youths hanging from the pillars, whose vital organs had not been hit by the firing squad, lifted his head and stared at his assassins. He spat out a thick ball of blood and cried out with all his waning strength:

"Assassins . . . cowards . . . *maricones.* Faggot soldiers."

The sergeant, whose coarse face was covered with boils and blackheads, flushed with rage; he flipped the safety catch from his black Galil and aimed it at the youth. From a distance of eight meters he failed to hit the young man, who regarded him with a contemptuous smile as the bullets, like drops of turpentine on water, became encrusted against the adobe wall of the municipality.

Still smiling, the youth shouted again, "Faggot soldiers . . . cowards!"

58

The commander scolded the sergeant: "Don't be an ass. Go stick it into the motherfucker's heart and shut him up once and for all."

Livid with hatred, the sergeant took out his double edged bayonet and sank it coldbloodedly into the youth's heaving chest, exactly on a level with his heart. Blood gushed instantly from his wound and sprayed the sergeant's face. The young man began to vomit up mouthfuls of bright red blood, writhing against the pillar like a mortally wounded jaguar.

Not satisfied, the enraged sergeant placed the barrel of his Galil against the man's temple and fired another blast.

"That's enough, get away!" shouted the commander, who had watched unflinchingly the demonic fury of his sergeant.

The perspiring executioner wiped the blade of his bayonet on the youth's pants and backed away from the lifeless body with a look of stone. He stood next to me and reclaimed from a soldier the end of the rope that hung around my neck. I felt the tremors pass through the rope and into my body, as the assassin's hand would not stop shaking.

The sergeant then suggested that I be disposed of as soon as possible.

"*Mi comandante*, do we get rid of this one, too?"

"Yes, but hold on, I want to make sure the others are dead." He approached the bodies hanging from the pillars, and lifted each one's head by his hair to verify with his own eyes that the "guerrillas" were indeed lifeless corpses.

After a careful examination, he stepped back and cooly crossed their names from the list: Antonio, Gaspar, José, Matías, Manuel, Ruperto.

One of the chiefs of the civil defense patrol approached the commander. "Forgive the intrusion, *mi comandante*, I would like to request that the families of the six dead civilian defenders be allowed to withdraw to their homes to mourn their dead – "

"Which civilian defenders?"

"The ones who fell in the outskirts of the village."

"How many were there?"

"So far, we know of six who are still lying where they fell; there are several others who have still not appeared."

"Only the women can go," he replied dryly.

In truth, it seemed a miracle that more defenders had not been killed in that surprise encounter between the army and the civil patrol.

The comander had started toward me when the soldier bearing the radio transmitter called him to say that the head of another military detachment wanted to speak with him.

After consulting his watch – it was five o'clock – the lieutenant turned back to answer the call. Since I was standing nearby I could hear the exchange, and I realized that one of the detachments based in my home town was calling in. I did not know what to think and had no idea how I would be disposed of when this other group of soldiers arrived on the scene.

Some of the leaders of the civil patrol who had fled when the shooting began had mistakenly informed the military at the base that the village was under attack from the guerrillas – so they had set out in search of them. That explained the imminent arrival of another military patrol to that ill-fated village.

As I looked around me I sensed the villagers' confusion as the women prayed aloud for the Lord's protection, and cried out in Mayan their grief and pain.

60

THE SECOND ARMY PATROL

The soldiers from town arrived shortly after. They wore a lighter shade of speckled green than the ones taken for guerrillas by the civil defenders. At their head was a young officer, short and light-skinned, and his soldiers also looked younger than the unshaven career veterans who had shattered the peace of our community. The two officers met and exchanged impressions.

"The hell with you all," said the older commander. "You were supposed to have covered this zone and cleared it of subversives. Look over there how many guerrillas we caught and disposed of today."

"And why not?" replied the younger lieutenant. "We already covered this village on August 30th, and executed two guerrillas."

"That's bull. You guys sit around the barracks and drink all day, and when you're called up to fight subversives, you stay put with your arms crossed. I was sent here to kill guerrillas, and that's just what I'm doing. You have to go look for the meat."

"That's just why we were here ten days ago," the other insisted, "and wasted two of the bastards. Isn't that so, *señores?*" he addressed the civil defenders closest to him.

"*Sí, mi comandante,*" they replied instantly.

"All right then," said the older commander, "so that you can see for yourselves how it's done, look at how we finished off those cowards."

Had others witnessed this scene, they might have had the same impression I did, that this demented officer killed only for the sake of killing, without the slightest understanding of what he was doing.

The younger officer and his soldiers still had some inkling of the value of life, and tried to avoid situations like this one so as not to stain their hands with innocent

61

blood. After all, they still had many years ahead of them to consider the consequences of their actions.

All military conscripts are trained to kill – only to kill – although not all of them follow orders with the same blind disregard for human life. I'd had the opportunity to witness the young officer's conduct on August 30th, when he had ordered the execution of two residents of the village.

On that occasion, a number of civil defenders had acted overzealously in ferreting out suspects from among their own neighbors. Under orders from their leaders, they prowled the vicinity like a pack of wolves after a scent, in search of subversives. Although most of the defenders participated out of fear, a few did it with the full intention of wiping out "the ones from the mountains."

"Communism is bad; they will take away our lands. We have to fight to protect our lands." This was said by a wretched youth who had no land of his own to cultivate, and whose only livelihood was to fetch water or gravel from the river bank. All the Indians of this area share their lands communally, in the traditional manner. The only landowners are outsiders who laid claims to tracts of land and took out documents. The vast majority live as their ancestors did, without private land ownership of any kind.

So it was with the civil defenders who apprehended two of their neighbors living in the outskirts of the village and took them, bound up with ropes, to the military base in town. One of the two captives kept a revolver hidden in a mound of trash in the patio of his house, and the other was seized for a similar suspicion.

One of them pleaded in his native tongue and insisted that he was innocent of any subversion. "My brothers, we are your own neighbors, why do you want to kill us? Look at my five children – have you no regrets at leaving them

62

orphaned? We have caused you no harm. Please understand."

"No, we promised not to release anyone who fell into our hands," replied one of the chiefs of the civil patrol. "Not even if it's our own father or brother."

This was the first time the civil defenders had begun speaking in these terms. How sad it is when a man loses his own identity and is easily indoctrinated! The defender was repeating to his own neighbor what the military had drummed into his head: Destroy, kill, even if it includes your own family. This military doctrine had gradually undermined the foundations of an indigenous culture, causing the Indian to act against his own will and best interests and destroying what is most sacred in his ancient Mayan legacy: love and respect for one's own neighbor, which translates into a policy of mutual support.

Despite all the pleas of the two captives and their wives, they were tied up and marched off toward the military base at about eleven in the morning on that August 30th, 1982.

About half-way to the town, one of the two managed to untie his hands and attempted to flee but the forty defenders caught up with him, beat him with their clubs, and then tied both of them up more firmly. They were determined to deliver them to the base.

The military officers congratulated the defenders for the capture, and set upon the two men, interrogating and kicking them brutally.

"So you were the ones causing trouble over there? Are you ready to show us where the real ones are hiding out?"

To avoid further torture, the captives said yes. A patrol of *kaibiles* immediately set out with the two men and the civil defenders.

The villagers were surprised to see the two neighbors arrive in the plaza, followed by the civil defenders and the platoon of *kaibiles,* who were armed to the teeth with high-caliber rifles and submachineguns.

It was about five in the afternoon when they passed through the village and began climbing up one of the steeper hills. The captives led them to a small cave that was completely empty.

The young officer who headed the platoon became furious and gathered all the villagers in the school patio.

"These two motherfuckers tried to pull a fast one on us. Instead of taking us to their cohorts, as they had promised, they led us to a cave where even a rat couldn't hide out. Now, they will pay the price for their deceit."

The two had evidently thought up the deception to gain time, but they had no chance to attempt an escape with so many defenders and soldiers on top of them.

The moon shone calmly as the defenders gathered in a circle around the two captives, as the officer instructed them to. He then yanked the younger of the two – Jesús by name – and yelled in his face: "All right, you. Tell us now, who are your *compañeros?* Speak up, shitface."

He did not reply. Jesús fixed both eyes on the ground, bit his lips and remained silent.

"All right, fucker. Since you won't answer, this is where you will die." The officer kicked him and ordered him to kneel, yanking on the end of the rope tied around his neck to force him to his knees.

He tried to stand up, but the officer kicked him in the gut, and he collapsed without uttering a sound. The villagers looked on at this scene as at something foreign to them. They all breathed heavily, causing them to sigh constantly.

"Now, recite the *pater noster,*" the officer ordered.

Jesús stammered the prayer.

"Louder, I can't hear."

Jesús ignored the officer's shrill tone of voice.

"Are you done?"

"Yes."

"All right. Now, *señores* defenders, I want you to execute these two subversives yourselves. You captured them, and now you must finish them off."

The villagers-turned-civil-defenders recoiled at following that unexpected order. Frightened, they looked at one another and drew back together.

"All right, you spineless scum. Why do you refuse to kill these two turds?"

One of the defenders spoke up: "Because we are not used to killing. We are Christians."

"Christians like the great whore's mother. You will now get used to killing or I will finish you off myself. Do you understand me?"

"Yes!"

"Or is it that you are the henchmen of these motherfuckers – is that why you won't kill them?"

"No!"

"All right, then, get it done!" The officer aimed his weapon at the vacillating patrol members.

A veteran civil defender, the most callous among them, stepped forward first and aimed a telling blow on the head of the first kneeling captive, Jesús. He was joined by the villagers who had planned the capture, and then by the others who formed the circle. They began to pummel the condemned villager with their polished clubs. He tried to scream, but all that came out was a horrendous gurgling of the blood in his chest.

The villagers stepped aside when their arms grew tired. The officer verified that the body lying in a pool of blood was still twitching, its chest heaving to take in air – and he repeated the order:

"You men feel sorry for this scum, and that's why he won't die. Once more, all of you go to it and get it done right."

The defenders returned to their macabre homicidal task, their assorted clubs and sticks dripping warm blood. The sounds produced by the blows that fell on the

65

luckless man's head and body were like those made by a cracked coconut. When the skull was beaten to a pulp and the face disfigured beyond recognition, the participants in the sinister drama stepped back once again to contemplate the horror.

But it was still not over. Mauled as he was, Jesús' body continued its contractions, as if his lungs were struggling to take in whatever oxygen was left in that dense atmosphere.

"This fucker doesn't want to die," the officer said drily. A soldier took out his knife and sank it casually in Jesús' throat, as he writhed in his death throes. The blood flowed in spurts as the soldier sawed at his trachea with the knife, already coated with thick, coagulated blood.

"Now it's done," the officer said, satisfied. He grabbed the other captive by the hair and paraded him before the men.

"All right, now you can amuse yourselves with this one."

Goyo, who was known in the community as a humble and servile type of person, looked frightened out of his wits by the circle of men, each standing with his blood-stained *garrote*.

The officer asked, "Do you know this man?"

"Yes, we know him, but he has lived among us only a short time. He is an outsider."

"I already gave the order to finish him, what are you waiting for?"

The defenders wasted no time in throwing themselves on the newcomer and beating him without respite. I suspect the first solid blow killed him, as he did not utter a single moan after the strangled "Ay!" that escaped his lips when the first blow dropped him to his knees.

When the executioners backed off, the officer verified that they had completed their work and nodded his approval.

66

From that day I knew the attitude of this new officer who had washed his hands of the crime, so that he could claim that the army does not kill, that it is the Indian defenders who are doing the butchering . . . How astute of him!

The defenders for their part showed their first pangs of remorse.

"I don't want either of these scum taken to the cemetery," the officer had said. "They deserve to be thrown to the vultures."

Some of the more compassionate villagers dug a shallow ditch next to the chapel and threw in the unwrapped bodies like dead dogs, then covered them with a few shovelfuls of earth. The events of that day were indelibly imprinted in the memory of the community, which feared that the spilling of blood would attract further calamities.

All of this had happened just ten days earlier, on August 30th.

The commander looked at me with disdain as he announced to the young officer, "And here is the little schoolmaster who has also been mixed up in trouble-making. We planned to drag him with us, but now that you've come, you may as well take him with you and dump him wherever you please. We will do the same to this other motherfucker that we will drag with us."

They referred to Matyax, the other villager whom they executed a few days later in the cemetery of a different municipio, to show the people there how they deal with enemies of the government.

The commander handed me over to the patrol, whose camouflage fatigues were of a lighter shade of green. I felt a glimmer of relief and hope because I knew the attitude of the younger officer to be somewhat calmer. There was also the possibility they would take me into town, where my family could find out about me and try to intercede with the military.

The time had flown. It was nearly six. The soldiers under the command of the ruthless older lieutenant flung their bulky sacks over their shoulders and prepared to evacuate. Their occupation of the village had been profitable as they had looted everything of value from the houses they searched.

One of the soldiers who had not taken part in the looting explained himself to me just before he left: "You should know that we have our own wives and children to feed, and so we were deceived into joining the army. It was against our wills that they armed us and sent us to the mountains to combat the guerrillas. The fifty dollars they pay us a month is not enough to support our families with. That's why they allow us to loot and steal, so we can supplement our meager wages. We were tricked into coming here. The officers tell us we Indians must do away with our own people because the Indians are enabling the guerrillas to carry out the revolution."

This was how the soldier explained their inhuman behavior in our community.

The *kaibiles* headed south, in the same direction from which they had come, without turning even once to look on the devastation they left behind or on the families they had damaged irreparably.

MARCHING IN THE DARK

The patrol in charge of me also prepared to depart for the military base. There were only twenty soldiers in the patrol, as opposed to eighty in the first group.

Several of the civil defenders were also readying to take two of their companions wounded in battle to the town hospital. They put on rubber boots and set off on the trail with their battery lamps.

September is the season of rains. I realized that the laces of my shoes would not withstand the heavy mud on the road, so I asked four acquaintances who were nearby if they would bring me some cord to secure the top of my shoes with. When they brought me the cord I asked them:

"Please, could you pick up my shoulder bag, which I already packed, and take it to town with you?"

"We'll take it with us, rest easy about that."

"And could you please let my wife know that I am being held captive. Maybe she can speak with someone in authority so they'll set me free . . ."

"Don't worry, we'll let her know as soon as we arrive, and may God be with you, brother." They set out ahead of the others.

The night spread relentlessly over mountain, roads and hillsides.

A soldier loosened the rope around my neck so the knot would not chafe. It was a few minutes past six. The sky was darkening, and it grew cold. The mist rose out of nowhere, and soon it began to drizzle.

An old friend approached me. "Is there anything I can do for you? I didn't dare speak with you because they would have beaten me."

"Don't worry about me, friend, and thank you for thinking of me."

"Have they taken some of your things already?"

"Yes, some other friends are doing it."

"Anything else you want?"

"A little water," I said, and he gave me his canteen to drink from. "Don't be afraid," he said again. "I am with you in your suffering."

I did not reply, but watched him slip his *morral* over his head, and walk quickly to catch up with the others.

"Forward . . . March," ordered the officer, and I was placed at the head of the column of soldiers. I turned for a last look and was saddened to see the villagers sunk in a profound sorrow. Hardly anyone said goodbye.

We began the ascent of Pacayales, which overlooks the picturesque village of Tzalalá, with its straw huts lost among the stone corrals, the orchards and fruit trees.

The narrow mule-trail twisted among boulders and slippery slabs of sharp stone that were barely visible in the dwindling light. I had trodden this same trail so often in my trips to the village that I knew every break and ditch by heart, and the intermittent lightning flashes in the darkened sky enabled me to make my way without stumbling.

A fine drizzle was falling, and a dense mist gathered above the hills. We were wrapped in a chill cottony embrace as we neared the summit of Pacayales. From here, on a clear day one has an enchanting view of the contours of the village of Tzalalá. I turned instinctively for a last look below, seeking out the mourning candles lit in the homes of the bereaved, but in the darkness and steady winds I could see nothing.

The young officer sat down on the wet grass by the roadside and ordered a halt.

"Corporal Nicolás, give the word that we're taking a break, and they can eat their rations."

The corporal passed the word on and everyone sat down on the grass or on a dry rock they made out in the dark. No one raised his voice or struck a match, for fear of alerting the guerrillas that might be lurking nearby.

They quietly zipped open their rucksacks and took out their tinned rations, which they wolfed down.

It was 7:30, and I realized I hadn't eaten a thing since dawn, but the sight of the soldiers sating their ravenous appetites did not waken the least hunger in me, as my sorrows eclipsed all physical desires. As we rested, the drizzle lightened, and the soldiers took out small towels to dry their faces, hands and necks. I rubbed the last rainwater from my hair and felt some drops slide under my collar. The cold must have been intense, but I did not feel it. This hill I normally climbed in forty minutes had taken us over an hour, and the strain to reach the summit had caused me to perspire and become overheated.

During the extended rest, however, the cold air dried my clothes, and they froze on my bare skin, chilling me to the marrow.

After he'd eaten, the lieutenant approached me and lit his cigarette, despite his earlier warning against striking matches. "All right, why were you captured?"

I replied calmly, "One of the accused villagers claimed to have heard my voice one night when two men were looking for him. He thought I had accused him of being a reactionary and I don't know what else."

"And you deny being one of the men who threatened him?"

"I certainly do. I can assure you that fellow was mistaken. Anyone can confuse two people's voices when they are uncertain, and that is what happened with him."

"In any event, we will talk this over tomorrow at the base, with the officer in charge."

"I hope he will understand my situation. I am a schoolmaster dedicated to my work, and I know nothing about what they accuse me of."

"We shall soon see," he said, and turned to speak with his men.

"Corporal Nicolás, prepare your men to depart."

71

"They are ready, *mi comandante*."

"Forward, then. And let the prof lead the way."

Once again I walked at the head as we began the descent of "Los Amates" slope. The dense mist shrouded the starlight, so I could barely see a step in front of me. The officer called out:

"Take care you don't lead us astray and make no attempt to escape, or we'll empty our cartridges on your fucking body."

"Understood," I replied, as I led them by feeling my way between the enormous boulders on either side of the road.

It was eight-thirty on my watch, which had a luminous dial, and we had yet to cover half the distance to town. I pictured the villagers who had gone ahead already resting in their relatives' homes while I trudged in the dark like a blind man, my feet steeped in mud and my toes bleeding inside my shoes.

The soldier who held the end of the rope tied around my neck collided with a jutting rock and sat down with a groan, letting go of the rope. I continued on my way as if I had not noticed. A little farther on the soldier caught up and leaned on my shoulder, and we continued until a narrow stretch made it impossible to walk two abreast. I then picked up the end of the rope and wound it around my arm.

With this advantage, and knowing the pitch darkness would work in my favor, I formulated a plan of escape. I could tell they were exhausted and would not be in any condition to chase after me. The only danger was in the volleys of rifle fire and the hand grenades the officer had threatened me with, when he anticipated the possibility of my escape. Ready for anything, I fixed on a place in the trail ahead of me where I could roll under a barbed wire fence into a small coffee orchard and then hide out in a ditch until the shooting let up.

As the moment approached my mind worked with astounding speed, and the prospect of success seemed so assured that I smiled in the dark. But when I was ten meters from the spot I suddenly changed my mind and gave up my plan. I knew I had every probability of getting away, but I would leave my family in a situation of great risk. What good was my freedom if my wife and children would have to pay the consequences? I decided to go to the base and face interrogation with my reasoned pleas of innocence. My nerves calmed down, and the thought of escape receded from my mind, like a turbid wind that had momentarily thrown me off balance.

I was hurting all over as we reached the main road into town, and the officer caught up with me. "Are you there, prof?" he called out.

"Yes, I am here."

"And who is holding the end of your rope?"

"No one, *mi comandante*. Here is the rope, if anyone wants to hold it."

"Well, it's no longer necessary since you evidently have no intention to escape."

"I have no reason to escape. I know I am innocent, and I have faith you will deal fairly with me."

I wished my words to reach deep into the young officer's conscience, but he made no reply and only asked how much farther we had before we reached town.

"About one and half kilometers, no more. We'll be there shortly."

We walked on until the lights of town came into view and grew steadily brighter. From afar we heard the sounds of the marimba. The echoes reached my ears by a moist breeze redolent of laurel.

We reached town about ten. I was overjoyed to arrive alive and in one piece in my beloved birthplace. More than once I had feared that they would dispose of me on the trail, or that a band of guerrillas would attack that

73

weary patrol in the dark. But it hadn't turned out that way.

The marimba was still playing in the community hall, but very few people walked the rain flooded streets. I wished the mist were denser, so that I would not reveal my disgrace to any acquaintances passing by who might recognize me. All I wanted at that moment was to see my wife and children, but there was no one waiting when we arrived in the park.

We finally reached the base. The soldiers standing guard at the entrance stepped aside when the patrol approached and took me inside with them. It was common knowledge that any civilian who entered was never seen alive again, and his fate would never be known. I stared at death in the barrels of the Galil rifles held by each of the soldiers standing guard.

INSIDE THE BARRACKS

On entering the barracks, a wave of sadness and pain overtook the optimism I had silently nurtured along the way. That place of green tents and barbed-wire barricades over six feet high was even gloomier in appearance than I had anticipated; a place in which so many lives had been snuffed out had to seem no less mournful than one of the many clandestine burial sites lost among the mountains.

I felt the wings of death flutter above my head as I entered like a sleepwalker in that cursed place. I wanted to weep, but once again was stilled by the knowledge that the Almighty alone could dispose of my life.

The young officer led me by the rope to one of the inner patios, then left me in the hands of five soldiers while he retired inside to have a drink. After he'd eaten and drunk his fill, he asked to see the military commander.

"The lieutenant is dancing in the salon," the soldiers replied.

"Very well. Keep an eye on this one until I get back. Place him over there, by the pillar."

The patrol officer left me at the mercy of lower-rank soldiers who were uninformed about my background and how I got there.

One of the first to comment was a short, dark sergeant whose eyes were inflamed from lack of sleep. He sneered at me and remarked aloud to the five soldiers who regarded me with a raw, vivid hatred:

"One more guerrilla they've brought us. We'll put this motherfucker away for good this very night." Before I could reply, he gave me a sharp blow in the gut that nearly broke something inside.

"Step back, faggot!" he snapped and shoved me until I was pinned against the corner pillar of that corridor. One

75

of the soldiers brought a rope and they tied my arms down, then wound the end several times around the pillar, securing it with a large knot. They did the same with the rope I still had around my neck; they pushed my head back, banging it against the pillar, then strapped me down so that I was totally immobilized.

Once I was pinned to the pillar so that my chest jutted out, the sergeant approached once more. "All right, you shitface guerrilla. What kind of arms did you carry?"

I made no reply to his question.

Infuriated, he slapped my face and drew blood from my mouth.

"Speak up, son of a bitch, or we'll force you to talk in any case. What kind of arms did you use?"

He looked at me with so much hatred that the spittle frothed in the corner of his mouth. Despite his fury, I did not cringe, but answered him evenly:

"I don't know what you're referring to; all I can tell you is that I am a Christian and therefore respect the lives of my fellows. I believe in the Fifth Commandment, 'Thou shalt not kill.'"

"Speak up, motherfucker!" he shouted, hitting me again in the face.

I looked down and saw the blood dripping from my nose, staining my blue chequered shirt. I maintained a hermetic silence.

"Look, I'll tell you what," he said. "just give us the names of one or two of your companions, and we'll let you go.

"*Señores*, I've already told you the truth," I replied. "I am a schoolmaster dedicated to my work. My wish is to contribute to the betterment of my homeland."

"You don't fool any of us with your high-sounding jabber. You can rest assured that you won't get out of here alive." And they turned and went out into the street.

I breathed deeply to offset the effects of the beating and tried to keep my legs from collapsing with fatigue. It was now midnight, and my thoughts flew toward my wife and children, who would be alone in our home, worried sick over my absence. My clothes were stiff from the mud and water and stained with blood: they clung heavily to my body, causing my muscles to tense so as to repel the cold that bit at the marrow of my bones.

Through the open flap of one of the tents I could make out the soldiers who had been on patrol; they had changed their uniforms and were drinking hot coffee from plastic cups. I wanted something warm inside me to feel human again, but the blows by the hysterical soldiers drove even the desire for hot coffee from my mind. Never had my head weighed so heavily on my neck, as I recalled the missed opportunity for escape. I became angry with myself for falling so stupidly into death's clutches.

Weary from going over in my head what I could have done at the opportune moment, I let myself go blank and wondered how my life would end on that night of September 9th. I spat out a thick glob of blood that slid down my nasal cavities, and then remained inert, in suspension, listening to my labored breathing.

A little while later there was a change of guard in the barracks, and the soldiers who were relieved came down the corridor. They shouted from boredom and spouted profanities as they passed the pillar to which I was bound like a criminal.

The first ones to walk by stared at me with hatred and disdain and, without the least constraint, drove their fists into my chest while others struck me in the abdomen, causing me to cringe with pain.

"Too bad this chicken won't live out the night," they taunted me with hate-filled eyes, thirsting for my blood. After hitting me they retired casually to their bunkbeds to undress, perhaps to sleep. I was horribly depressed. I was exposed to the elements and to any passing sadist with an impulse to lash out with a swift kick, a fist in the face or a rifle-butt in my belly. I felt like weeping, but I held back once more. I had to gather my strength so as not to buckle under. My bones felt cracked and pulverized from the chills that coursed up and down my body.

It was one in the morning, and I began to count ahead in my mind . . . two, three, four, five . . . sunrise. Still trusting in Divine Providence, I thought the new day might bring an improvement in my situation, unless, of course, they killed me that very night.

Time passed so slowly that one-thirty a.m. crept by, laden with my sighs and recollections of happier times. The dancing in the salon was coming to an end, for I heard the footsteps of the officers echoing in the corridor. They laughed boisterously, joking and gossiping and swaggering like real he-men with the beer and alcohol swelling their bellies.

And now my fear increased, for I knew these military men who were so sanguine when sober, would be capable of unimaginable bestial acts under the effects of alcohol.

To my surprise, the first one I saw was the young officer who had brought me here from the village. From a distance I smelled the beer and tobacco on his breath and recognized the self-confident smile of one who knows himself to be "a proud officer of the army."

He weaved slightly as he approached the pillar I was yoked to. "What happened, prof? Why have they tied you up like that?"

"The ones you left in charge of me beat me like savages," I said. The moderation he had shown earlier encouraged me to speak frankly with him and almost without fear.

"These stupid bastards always do the opposite of what they're ordered to," he said. "But don't worry, I'll have you set free right away." He called over a soldier and said firmly. "All right, I want this guy untied."

The soldier leaned his rifle against the stone barrier that divided the patio from the corridor and began to undo the thick knots that bound my waist to the pillar and pressed painfully against my throat.

As soon as he loosened the knots I rubbed my stiff fingers that were purple from the cold. After untying me, the soldier made an attempt to reassure me:

"Don't worry too much. They'll let you go tomorrow, because otherwise they would have taken you to the dungeon below with the other captives. They're much worse off."

"I hope to God you're right," I said.

The soldier called to the lieutenant, who had gone inside to write some messages, "Should I remove the ropes from his neck?"

"Yes, take them all off and then put him in the salon so he can find a place to sleep."

"Let's go inside," the soldier said, and I followed him like a starving and filthy beggar, eager to curl up in some out-of-the-way corner and wrap himself in trash or anything else he can find that will keep the cold from freezing his bowels. I understood then why beggars love their treasure trove of old and ragged things and why they sleep with one eye open to protect them at night, and why they guard them so jealously during the day. Whatever beggars have, beggars love. Those tattered bags full of fruit waste and rotting leftovers are precisely what I craved that night.

"Stay here," the soldier said, pointing to the cold tile floor. I sat down beside a large tin container that had been placed below a steady drip of rainwater through a poorly laid tile in the roof. The leaking raindrops did not splatter on the floor, but fell in the exact center of the tin, producing a dull, monotonous sound.

The place the soldier picked out for me to lie down in faced the main portal, which was kept open so that a moist, frigid draft lashed my face.

I did not bemoan my fate. At least I was still alive and had some hope of being rescued. I waited anxiously for

79

morning and news of my wife, who would surely have made efforts to have me set free and would by now have approached influential persons in town to intercede for me.

In the midst of my whirling thoughts and hopes I momentarily shut my eyelids, not because I was sleepy, but because my eyes smarted from the cigarettes the soldiers smoked as they lay on their green bunkbeds.

The coarse idiom of these brutes was unmoderated by the lateness of the hour. "Who the fuck took my blanket?" one of them yelled.

"Your whore of a mother," another replied.

"Shut up, motherfuckers, turds, and let me sleep," grumbled a third from a corner.

Seated on the cold floor, I reclined my back against the wall as the cold winds outside continued to blow.

THE NIGHT OF DREAD

It was two a.m. when I checked my watch again. Most of the soldiers were asleep, and the few standing guard in the patio and corridor laughed and cursed in shrill voices that failed to perturb the placid sleep of their fellows, who lay inert on their bunkbeds with their Galil rifles by their sides.

I was surprised to see the young officer enter the salon at that late hour, accompanied by several of his men.

"Haven't you slept yet?" he asked me.

"*No, mi comandante.* I am not sleepy."

"You need not be afraid to sleep."

"Thank you. I will try to lie down."

He stripped a blanket from an unoccupied bed and flung it at me. "Here, use this to cover yourself." I caught it in the air so it would not fall into the puddle beside me. With trembling hands I flung it over myself to cover my painful lungs.

"Lie down and wrap yourself in it," he insisted, "and don't be concerned about soiling it."

I replied, "I am so covered with mud I would rather not lie down. I can sleep sitting up."

The officer fetched me a plastic raincoat so I could place it under me on the floor. I thanked him, and he went out with the other soldiers. I stretched out on top of the raincoat and wrapped myself in the blanket.

Before I could fall asleep another officer came in from the street and bent over me. When he flung off the blanket for a closer look, I saw that he was more drunk than his predecessor, and he also looked belligerent.

"Who the shit are you?" he said, kicking my right side with his boot. I stood up at once to prevent his kicking me again.

"I am a schoolmaster," I told him.

"And what the fuck are you doing here? Are you a civil defender, or what?"

"I have been a defender, but now I am here because of a case of mistaken identity."

"Whose mistake was it?"

"Well, a villager who was killed by the soldiers accused me of having threatened him one night–" I began, but he did not let me finish.

"Look, fucker, if you've been mixed up in subversive crap, this is no place for you to sleep. You, men – " he ordered several of his followers – "take this turd and throw him in the pit. Let him spend the night there."

"Yes, lieutenant sir," they replied, and lifted me by the arms, then dragged me outside, past the pillar I had been tied to and across the patio to the rim of a foul cesspool filled with mud, water and garbage. As they held me at the rim I heard a muffled cry rise from the depths and a head broke the surface, struggling to free itself from that horrible captivity.

I could not make out the features of that unhappy wretch, who screamed with clenched teeth from the edge of that pit, exposed to the cold night wind and freezing rain.

"T–t–take me out or shoot me, but don't leave me in here," he wailed pitifully.

One of the soldiers leaned over the rim the man was clinging to and hit him in the face with his rifle butt, sinking him once again into the dark murky waters of the pit. "Shut up, turd."

The soldiers hesitated before tossing me in head first because it occurred to them that the two of us together might attempt to escape.

The bigger one said, "Go ask the officer if we should take the other prick out of the pit first, or if both of them should soak together."

The other soldier went to ask his superior what they should do with me and came back shaking his head.

82

"What did the commander say?" the first soldier asked.

"He was already snoring, and I did not want to wake him. I spoke with the other one, who got pissed as hell."

"Well, asshole, what did he say?"

"Well, he got real pissed and yelled, 'Why the fuck are you carrying out your own orders with that prisoner?' And then he said this motherfucker is in his charge, and we are to put him back where he left him."

"The great whore's mother, how I hate these counter-orders. They've got us coming and going like ninnies. Well, what the fuck, orders are orders."

Visibly angry, they returned me to the salon, and I sat down again on the plastic raincoat while the soldier threatened me:

"If you try to escape, shitface, you won't even get as far as the corridor, so stay very quiet if you value your life."

Before they withdrew they placed two rifles at either side of me, leaning against the wall. I suspected it was a trap to see if I would reach for one of them in an attempt to escape; they would then have riddled me with bullets without a qualm. I stared at the black Galils with their long curved cartridge clips and thought about how many people were killed with those weapons.

All at once a piercing scream tore through my thoughts and caused my heart to pound violently; it was like a howl from the world beyond. The soldiers had become so inured to these hair-raising screams, not one of them stirred in his bunk. They all kept on snoring, impervious to what was happening in the adjoining torture chamber.

The wails of the unfortunate man got lost in the night's sepulchral silence. The barking of dogs in nearby houses was the only response to the bone-chilling howls, which died down gradually, like a radio whose volume is lowered little by little until it is soundless. I shuddered to think of the fate of that luckless man after they finished

83

with him. First they cut out one eye, then the other. Then the nose, lips, the tongue, ears and testicles, and at last they slice off his head. It is a slow, excruciating death, conceived to make a human being die in the greatest possible pain.

Again I felt like weeping – and I recalled the words of an old townswoman who commented on the assassinations and tortures: "Oh Lord, pity those who commit these crimes, who pretend death does not await them as well; but every hog has his Saturday, and who knows what price they will pay for causing this suffering and injustice. They pretend to be gods who pass judgement on the lives of these poor people . . ."

"Be quiet, Doña Petronila," her neighbors warned. "It is not prudent to speak so openly."

"What have I got to fear? Let them come and kill me. After all I am an old woman. The ones I feel sorriest for are all the young people they are carrying off and butchering without the least pang of conscience."

Old women like Doña Petronila, who stand up for what they believe, are scarce in our town.

The screams of that night have become forever engraved in my memory. I thought disconsolately on all the horrendous crimes that have been committed since the army set up a base in our town.

The incinerated corpses of the victims are thrown into a pit the military dug on the edge of a nearby ravine. "Forbidden Zone – No Trespassing," read the signs they put up, to prevent people from stumbling on the clandestine cemetery that has grown day by day in our community.

I did not shut my eyes for an instant during the remainder of the night, for fear they would catch me off-guard and assassinate me. Footsteps were still audible in the corridor, but all was silent in the large hall where I sat, waiting.

My watch showed two-thirty when other howls rose up from the far end of the barracks. This fueled my suspicion that a number of other prisoners were kept gagged and bound below, hidden away from the townspeople. They were dealt with only in the hours before dawn when the town was asleep and no one would be aware that this was a center for torture and other barbarities. But the townspeople knew, nonetheless.

A few of the luckier captives had escaped torture by managing to flee under the noses of their captors, but many others had been caught and cut down with machineguns.

For those who have to die, it is far better to be shot attempting to escape than to be killed slowly, staring up at your executioners' faces as they cut you open.

Fernando, a poor neighbor of ours and father of six children, was cruelly tortured and then decapitated. They removed his teeth one by one and forced him to swallow them, like hard pellets. They cut off his tongue, pierced his eyes. Yet he died bravely, like a man.

That night of September 9th was for me like a horrendous nightmare from which by a miracle I awoke with my life, unlike those unfortunates whose last exhalations were punctuated by agonizing howls.

Although I had not eaten since the morning of the previous day, I did not feel the slightest hunger from the moment I was taken prisoner until the following dawn. But I was affected by the intense cold of that night and by the chill dampness of the clothes that the heat of my body could not dry.

I recalled the youth in the pit, who had been less fortunate than I. His reactions were already those of a madman, and by now his body must have been eaten away by the corrosive muck. Or perhaps he was done in by the rifle butt the soldier shoved in his face, splitting open his forehead. Why was it, I repeatedly asked myself, that the soldiers harbor so much hatred in their hearts and behave so drastically toward their own people, while obeying the criminal orders of their superiors? Most of these men who kill and maim come from the same remote villages and belong to the same wretchedly poor families as do the condemned ones with whose blood they have stained their hands.

A friend who is an ex-soldier had told me one afternoon, not long before: "They brainwash and indoctrinate us in such a way that we could torture our own parents, if we were ordered to. I spent three years in the barracks, and what did I learn? Fucking zero. The only thing you are taught is to kill and kill, again and again. Just because you're fed well and warm blood runs in your veins, you soon want to start making the bullets fly, as if to say, it makes you feel real macho and no one can stand in your way. In my case, for example, during my time in the barracks I was always spoiling for a brawl, and if one didn't happen, I would go out looking for it. Just imagine."

I realized I was nodding off, and quickly rubbed saliva on my lids, fearful that I might have talked in my sleep and given away my friend's confession. When I checked my watch again, it was only four a.m. It seemed that time was standing still so as to make that night even harder to bear.

An hour and a half until sunrise, I said to myself, and I covered my weary shoulders with the blanket, to protect my aching lungs. I did not shut my eyes – on the contrary, I kept fully alert until dawn.

A NEW DAY

Crouched on the cold tile floor, I saw the first light of day advance slowly through the northern portal. The streetlights across from the barracks lost their brilliance as dawn cast its fiery sparks on the foothills of the Sierra Madre, the Cuchumatanes. In town, the *nixtamal* mills began to grind corn and flour, stirring the neighbors from their sleep.

I praised the Lord in his Omnipotence and thanked Him for permitting me to behold the light of a new day.

The intense cold lingered in the salon, whose doors had remained open all night long. At a few minutes past six the soldiers began to stretch lazily and rise from their wooden bunkbeds, which were arranged in double rows that covered the length and width of the decaying old building. In the patio, the morning sounds grew louder. Whistles, songs, exchanges of insults and profanities filled the premises. I rose from the floor, shook out the raincoat, and folded the blanket that had helped me fend off the worst of the night's chill.

I craned my neck to gaze out the main portal at the eastern horizon and the hazy blue peaks that cut their silhouettes against it.

In one corner of my narrow frame of vision, above the soldiers' green tents, a lone black vulture wheeled in the clean blue space, softly flapping its broad wings and moving its head from side to side, in search of carrion or perhaps a place to land. The *zopilote* was high up in the sky when I caught sight of him and slowly dropped until it broke its descent on some tree near the rim of the canyon that encircles our town. The casual freedom of that bird made me ponder my situation. At times one is filled with the same longings one had as a child. How I wanted to fly! To recover my freedom and wander over the infinite, released from worries, threats and oppression. I thought how winged creatures are the most beautiful in the world. May no one subjugate them and cause them to suffer the pains of injustice and imprisonment we humans are subject to.

Daybreak meant for me a reawakening of hope; it made me realize the sanctity of life. At other times I had watched the start of day with indifference, as a routine event. Now I began to understand why the sun sets and the sun rises, why there must be night before there can be dawn. What joy I felt to see the sunburst of colors light up the distant eastern sky beyond the Sierra Madre, the Cuchumatanes, far beyond the borders of Guatemala.

By the light of day I saw that my clothes and my body were coated with mud and bloodstains.

The soldiers made their bunks and swept the floor of the large hall before fetching their breakfasts from the kitchen. I recognized each of them as they passed the door; the first were the members of the patrol that had escorted me here, and behind them came the ones who had beaten me. In the light of day they seemed less fierce than they had last night. They all appeared young in comparison with the callous veterans who had murdered the youths in the village the day before.

Seated on the floor, I watched the officers enter and leave the hall like green venomous hornets.

One of the soldiers who entered with his breakfast approached me and said, "Here, prof, have some of this corn broth."

"*Gracias amigo*," I said, taking the small tin cup between my hands. I drank down the warm *atole* in no time and wished for one, two or more cupfuls of the revivifying broth, but no one offered me any.

I thanked God that not every soldier was malevolent and devoid of human feelings. His gesture made me understand that in their own way – although they dare not say so – they too are victims of a violence that has become institutionalized.

After I gulped down the dregs of *atole* at the bottom of the cup, I began to feel more like a real person. I rubbed my cheeks to make the warmth return. The night's bitter cold had numbed my nerves and muscles, and only now did my body begin to relax and recover its normal heat.

The soldiers passed by without hitting or addressing me. Despite the change in their bestial attitudes, I still felt desolate in their midst, like a mouse caught in a deadly maze.

Just before seven the young officer entered and asked, "Have you eaten anything, prof?"

"Yes, a cup of *atole* they gave me."

"That's not enough. You should eat something more."

"Don't concern yourself, that will do."

"Don't you believe it. Hey you, bring this fellow some food," he ordered the soldier in charge of sweeping the floor.

I seized the opportunity to ask the officer, "When will I be able to speak with the base commander to clear up my situation so I can be with my wife and children?"

"He'll be here shortly. Don't despair and don't let fear get to you."

"*Gracias, mi comandante*, I trust in you," I said.

I hoped in some way to influence the officer – to persuade him to mediate in my favor when the questioning began.

The soldier came back with a plate of tortillas and beans, but I still had no appetite and forced myself to swallow a few mouthfuls which barely went down my knotted throat.

The beans were hard and the tortillas were thick, but I ate several mouthfuls while keeping an eye on the large door through which the soldiers entered and exited. Among them was the officer who had ordered me placed in the pit. He looked at me with indifference and asked, "What are you doing here?"

"Waiting to speak with the base commander."

"He is having his breakfast. And they have brought you food?"

"*Si, gracias.*"

"That's good," he replied.

He turned casually and left for his work detail, like a tame dog, the very opposite of how he had behaved toward me the previous night.

Another soldier approached me with a thermos bottle in his hands. "Look, your wife has sent you this coffee . . ."

I leaped to my feet as though propelled by a spring. This meant my wife was just a few steps away from me, and I thought by craning my neck outside the door I could see her. I attempted it at once, but the barrier was higher than my line of vision and prevented me from seeing beyond the corridor. I accepted the thermos and a proper china cup, anxious to have news of my family.

"Have my children come with her?" I asked the soldier.

"Yes, three children have accompanied her and are sitting across the street on the bench to the left of the door."

I had the impulse to run out that instant and embrace my wife and children, but the sentinels at the door watched me closely, following my every movement.

Without being aware of it, tears welled up in my sleepless eyes. "Children!" I blurted out. "My little children, may the Lord keep you from becoming orphaned at such a tender age! How sad it must seem to you that 'Papa' has not come home bringing you candy and fruit."

I wiped my eyes with my shirtsleeves and pleaded with the soldier. "Look, please do me the favor to tell my wife to talk with the civil and church officials so they can intercede for me . . . And tell her that for the moment I am all right."

Drink your coffee, and I'll deliver your message when I return her the thermos."

I drank down two cups of hot coffee and returned the bottle to the soldier. He slung his rifle over one shoulder and went out the main portal.

I waited anxiously for his return. Sunk deep in thought, I cleaned the mud from under my fingernails. The proximity of my wife and children felt like a protective halo around me. I pictured them with sad and pleading eyes as they told the soldier of their need to see me and have me at their side.

The soldier returned shortly and smiled at me. "Your wife says she already spoke this morning with the persons you mentioned; you should stop worrying. You'll certainly get out of here alive and wagging your tail."

That news gave me renewed hope. For the first time in these endless hours I felt a lightening of my sorrowful burden. I knew now that attempts were being made to rescue me, and I had not been abandoned like the poor wretches who at two in the morning had wailed their agony for the last time.

I checked my watch and it was eight a.m. Time crawled at a snail's pace, and the thick air in that cold, gloomy building nearly choked me with its violent odor of body waste and assorted filth.

All the soldiers had left except for one who lay in his cot with his left arm in a plaster cast that was tied to his shoulder with a red kerchief.

"Don't feel so sad," he called aloud, jarring me back to my senses.

"I am not sad," I lied.

"I have a Bible here, in case you're interested."

I went over and sat down on the edge of his bunk, amazed that a soldier would have a Bible under his pillow.

"Here, take it, " he said, and passed me his Bible, which was bound in blue cloth. "I carry it with me everywhere, on my parents' advice."

"That's good," I said.

"You came here last night?"

"Yes, I had the misfortune to be taken for someone else."

"And did they beat you badly?"

"Some," I said, "but it doesn't matter."

"There are brutes here who enjoy beating people up. I am not one of them. When the beatings start, I step to one side and let the others do it. What good is it to hit some poor soul who for one reason or another has fallen into our hands?"

"I wish all of you felt that way," I said.

Our conversation was interrupted at that moment by a soldier who walked in with a pencil and a sheet of paper.

"What is your name?" he shouted at me.

I gave him my name slowly, and spelled it out.

"Aren't you A.C.?" He mentioned a name I had never heard before as he studied me maliciously.

"No. Here is my identity card if you want proof."

"I don't need it."

I asked him, "Can you tell me when I will be allowed to speak with the base commander?"

"That is difficult," he said. "It seems you know many things, and I think they will force you to talk. I suggest you cooperate and tell everything you know."

Having delivered his message, he left hurriedly. It was eight-thirty in the morning of Saturday, September 10th 1982.

"Don't betray any fear or let them catch you shaking," the soldier with the plaster cast warned me.

"If you owe nothing, you have nothing to fear," I said to him.

92

I lay down on an empty bed and opened the Holy Script to the Psalms of David. As I read and meditated on them I felt a surge of peace and calm. I was overjoyed to have the Bible in my hands, and from that moment I trusted even more in the power of God and felt renewed certainty that I would come out alive from this ordeal.

WITH *EL COMANDANTE*

I awoke with the Bible in my hand. I rose from that strange bed and rubbed my inflamed eyes with the side of my hand. According to my watch, it was eighteen minutes to ten. Overcome with fatigue, I had fallen asleep and lost all track of time.

In my dreams I had seen my oldest boy, seven years old, enter the barracks unseen by the soldiers, and after stroking my face he had untied me and led me outside by the hand. As we walked along the corridor, I realized he was no longer my son but my brother, who had been killed the year before.

"They will see us," I said to him

"No. They are blind and see nothing."

"But how can we go out the gate undetected by the guards?" I insisted.

"The gate is not there, and we can go out into the street with no trouble."

"And where shall we go?"

"Nowhere. We will just go home and remain there. They can't see me, but you are visible, and I will have to cover you from their sight."

He took me by the hand and let me out the heavily guarded gate without anyone seeing us. Once on the street . . . I woke up.

The dream had been so swift and beautiful, I could not forget it. I sighed heavily and closed the Bible that lay open on the bed.

Ten a.m. Time was slipping by, and I began to despair. The horror of spending another night in the barracks began to infect my thoughts.

It was then I became aware of the commanding officer hovering near the entrance, peering in at me.

95

This officer was tall, rather thin and very reserved. He wore a white sport shirt that contrasted sharply with his camouflage fatigues. His round, shaven face expressed dead seriousness, but it did not inspire as much fear as that of the officer who had ordered the village massacre. I saw him as in a dream at first, but his very real presence was watching me fixedly.

Still, his presence did not provoke the same turmoil in me, as he came in without a show of fury, quiet and unarmed, wearing that white sport shirt.

A face often betrays a person's nature, and that officer's attitude seemed more restrained than violent. This first impression I had of him helped me to gather strength for the interrogation still to come.

"Come with me," he said without speaking, simply gesturing with his fingers. I slipped the Bible under the bedsheets of the wounded soldier and quickly followed the officer the full length of the corridor to the far end of the building.

I feared he would lead me to a closed chamber where I would be made to "talk," as I had been warned, but instead the lieutenant stopped next to the rear door and leaned against the wall.

"What is your name?" he asked.

I gave him my name and resolved within myself to remain calm and reply to his questions confidently and without vacillation.

"Where do you live?"

"Here in town."

"And what did you do in the place where they caught you?"

"I work in the public school of that village."

"You're a schoolmaster, then?"

"Yes, I am a teacher of primary school and have been working for the Education Department for ten years."

"What do you know of the guerrillas?"

96

"Nothing. Absolutely nothing, Lieutenant sir. I am an honest person who is dedicated to his work; I know nothing of matters unrelated to my work."

"How many times have you set traps for the army?"

"I know nothing of what you're asking me. I told you I am a schoolmaster and work within a strict schedule. I have hardly enough time to prepare the lesson plans for my pupils."

"But if you've been accused, then you must be mixed up in troublemaking. You'd better tell me the truth."

"The one who accused me said my voice was similar to that of a man who had threatened him one night; you know, Lieutenant sir, that mistakes of this kind are easily made. I even asked him to back his accusation with some evidence and to expose whatever illegal activities he accused me of taking part in – participation in the guerrilla – but he was unable to do so. He was lying."

"But someone else is also accusing you." He gave me a hard stare, but I did not back down.

I said instead, "Look, I'll speak openly with you. One year ago army soldiers shot down my brother in the park, in plain view of the entire town. The army then accused him of being a guerrilla, although the plain truth is the soldiers had been drinking, and my brother was shot at random. Anyone in town can tell you that. Ever since then I have lived in fear of the army because anyone could make trouble for me simply by saying I am a subversive who seeks to avenge his brother's death. It is understandable that anyone who wished me harm would seize this opportunity to accuse me, as you said someone has. But I am sincere in saying to you that I am not one to seek revenge. I have put it all behind me and left it in the hands of Divine Justice.

"And now what do you plan to do?"

"To go on working in my little school, because in that way I help my homeland, and contribute to the peace and well-being of Guatemala."

"I know that if I set you free, you will go off and hide somewhere."

"Don't believe it, *mi comandante*. I have no reason to flee, as I don't owe anything to anyone. This is my town, this is my homeland, and I intend to remain here."

"You speak very prettily, but I hope you will back up what you say with actions."

"All I ask is that you give me an opportunity."

"All right then . . . But have you noted anything unusual in town, or do you know any persons who behave suspiciously?"

"No, *mi comandante*. I am here only on weekends and do not concern myself with other people's lives."

"You're lying . . . Didn't you just say you belong to this town?"

"I come from here, but my work obliges me to spend all week long in a village several kilometers' distance."

"And there in your village there are many guerrillas, is that right?"

"I have never seen them. The people in my village are peaceful; they are all farmers and fieldworkers."

"All right. I will put you to work. I want you to report to me every person that you think may be involved with the guerrillas."

After saying this, he looked at me fixedly. This was the condition I had feared hearing from the start. To denounce! This time I did not answer as readily as I had resolved to. This was a delicate situation in which I had no desire whatever to become an accomplice. I know well that to accuse or denounce someone is exactly the same as to kill him.

"What are you thinking? Will you do it or not?"

"I will see," is all I said. If I said flat out that I did not agree to that condition, I would never be allowed to leave that place alive.

"There is another condition," he said.

I feared it would be worse than the first.

"You must present yourself here in the barracks every day. If you do not comply with these conditions, you know very well what awaits you. But tell me first where you live."

"I live a good distance from here."

"In what block, neighborhood or zone?"

"In this same zone, only more to the south."

"But you are not making things clear. Give me some point of reference by which to find your house."

My evasions were useless, as that officer was determined to know where I lived. I began to fear a future kidnapping. I gave him my address, but mixed in some confused directions.

"One final question: Are you acquainted with J. R.?

"Yes, I have seen him on occasion here in town."

"Is he your friend?"

"No. I hardly have time to leave my house, and so I know many people only by sight, including him."

"Well, for your information he was a guerrilla and is resting peacefully in the bellies of some vultures below town."

I made no reply. Everyone in town knew of the disappearances of a number of their neighbors, but no one said anything, and I saw no reason to open my mouth and provoke more questions.

"I will expect you today at six in the evening. You have to be punctual in obeying my orders, or we will come to your house to get you. You may rest assured of that."

"At your orders, *mi comandante*. I will be here at six sharp, without fail."

"All right, you can go on home."

"Thank you, *mi comandante.* May I go out the rear door?"

"Whatever you wish."

At last the hoped-for moment had arrived, and I was leaving in one piece. I could still feel the chafing of the noose around my neck, but when I reached up to loosen it, I realized it was the wounds that were festering.

I took a few steps toward the back door and stopped to look over one shoulder. The commander was leaning against one of the pillars, looking at me. I then hurried to leave that place at once, fearful of getting a bullet in my back.

The guards stood firm and clutched their weapons when they saw me approach the door. I had the impulse to run full speed when I saw their menacing postures, but I restrained myself so as not to commit a fatal error. If I broke into a run they would take me for a fugitive and shoot me at once. I walked out the gate at my normal pace, acutely aware of my filthy, blood-stained clothes.

It was ten-thirty that Saturday morning when I emerged into a deserted street. I encountered only one or two townspeople who looked at me with curiosity and surprise. As soon as I turned the corner, no one could have prevented my swift flight toward home. I felt master of my fate once more and inhaled deeply the fresh and perfumed air of freedom.

With quickened steps I passed by some kids playing marbles in a large patio. They started up in alarm when they saw me. They must have thought I was some madman or drunkard who had been rolling in the mud.

OBEYING INSTRUCTIONS

When I arrived home, there was no one there. I burst into tears and then looked up at the wall where a picture of my dead brother looked down, smiling at me.

A knock at the door. "May I come in?"

I wiped my face and dried my tears. I did not want anybody to see the depth of my desolation.

"Come in."

A young woman, a neighbor named María walked in. "Dear God, you've come back!" she exclaimed. "Are you all right?"

"I am well, thanks."

"Here, I brought you some medicine; take it and it will calm you down."

"Thank you, María, I appreciate it."

"Your wife and children are praying in the church and may not know you're here. If you wish, I can send one of my boys to fetch them."

"Yes, please, I beg of you."

She prepared the medication and gave it to me to drink. Other neighbors arrived and wanted to know what had happened to me, but I had lost my voice. I did not wish to recall or relive a single instant of my ordeal, and so I confined myself to saying that very little had happened.

I was changing my clothes when my family arrived. I took my wife in my arms, weeping, and kissed her and my dear children for a long time. My feelings at that moment were indescribable. Death had been hovering over my shoulder, and I had feared I would never see them again. I understood it to be a miracle that I was still alive, and for that reason I felt immensely grateful to the Virgin, who had shielded me throughout that nightmare of screams, bullets, blood and death.

At six in the evening I presented myself at the barracks.

"Come back tomorrow at eight a.m.," they told me.

On September 11th a large number of villagers had arrived in town, and I learned that the bodies of those killed by the army had been buried at three in the afternoon on Saturday. The community had suffered the worst calamity in its history, and the relatives of the fallen had wept inconsolably day and night.

Many villagers, among them men, women and children had fled that Friday afternoon during the army's assault, and they returned to their homes two days later, battered and bruised from having hidden out two nights in the *barrancos* and rocky ravines.

A woman I know had gotten a bullet in her hand while she was making tortillas in her kitchen. An old man of seventy lay dying in his house after a beating by the soldiers who broke his jaw.

A youth of sixteen complained of a hole in his left ear where a stray bullet had pierced it. Other youngsters had their arms broken by the gunfire.

Ever since the death of my brother, I had not enjoyed a peaceful night's sleep. One of the army's tactics was to spring kidnapings after dark, usually between eleven and three in the morning. During those hours I remained on the alert, always ready to run out on hearing the barking of dogs at a stranger's approach.

After three I would drift off to sleep until dawn. My friends would warn me: "Be very careful. It's best not to sleep in your home because you never know what these men are plotting."

All of these things began under the administration of Romeo Lucas García, when the military, paramilitary, police and parapolice units kidnapped, tortured and killed anyone who might be a leader or who had any influence in town, and that included priests and catechists. I was now experiencing first hand all this violence unleashed against the poorest Indian communities of Guatemala.

On Sunday September 11th, at eight a.m., I presented myself at the military barracks as I had been ordered to do by the *comandante.* My wife and children accompanied me to act as my shield, and I did not neglect to pray to the Virgin as I had been doing and still continue to do.

I arrived at the main gate and informed the guard on duty of my reason for being there.

"The *comandante* will be right here. Wait for him."

My wife withdrew to sit on the bench across the street while I waited alone at the gate. Five minutes later the *Comandante* showed up, dressed the same way as the day before except that he had a pistol in his holster.

"Come inside," he said.

I entered with the same fear I had felt the first time. I followed five steps behind him, and we sat at the base of a wall under construction that would encircle the barracks.

The lieutenant regarded me with his customary seriousness and asked, "What news do you bring me?"

"None. I've only come to present myself as you requested."

"Very well. But today I'd like to speak with you at noon, because a man is coming to identify you."

He stared fixedly into my eyes, as if trying to guess my thoughts on hearing this grim announcement.

The sergeant in charge of torture approached ill-humoredly and looked at me obliquely, his large black eyes charged with hate and malice.

'These two are trying their psychological tricks on me,' I thought, and returned their fixed looks without blinking. I then replied firmly, with conviction.

"I'll be here at noon, just as you say."

"But don't run out on me."

"I have no reason to run away. I want to see this person who insists on perjuring me."

"I will await you, then."

I rose from my seat and went out quickly. My wife awaited me anxiously outside. Once I was alone with her I pondered the comandante's words. Was it possible the lieutenant who carried out the massacre in the village had returned to insist on my judgment? Or was some malevolent person simply trying to get rid of me?

"Don't worry, God and the Virgin will look after you," my wife said.

I spent the ensuing hours sunk in dark thoughts. Large tears rose to my eyes. To live like this, a plaything subjected to the whims of these people was not easy for a man with my yearnings for peace and justice and freedom. I did not know how long I could withstand it. I had my pride as a man of conscience, and, at whatever cost, I had to endure with dignity the intense pressures I was being subjected to.

At the appointed time I showed up at the barracks with a calmness that astounded even me. I don't know where I found the courage to confront those human beasts. I felt firm and certain of what I was doing. I had faith in God and confidence in myself and faced up defiantly to the death that menaced me from all sides.

"I have come to keep my appointment," I informed one of the guards.

"I'll go tell the *comandante*," he said.

I pinched the palm of my hand to ward off a nervous tremor that threatened to take possession of me.

The soldier returned shortly, followed by the commander.

"*Buenas tardes, mi comandante*," I shouted from afar, as if by greeting him courteously I could soften his heart toward me.

He approached me without responding. When he continued to stare at me without speaking, I said, "I have come just as you told me."

"Well, the man didn't come, you'd better return at six this evening."

"Just as you say, *mi comandante*."

Without another word, he withdrew.

I ran out like a deer, relieved and determined to go on living. I was overcoming step by step each of my old fears. These men could trick me with lies and false accusations and a thousand ruses they thought up themselves, but as long as I remained firm and serene, they could not make me fall easily into their traps. I would suffer with patience and humility.

Hoping to chase away the dark birds pecking away at my poor weakened head, I went for a stroll with my children that afternoon. I wanted to let the army and the townspeople know that I was not about to flee from anyone or anything.

At six in the evening I left for the barracks. The guard at the gate went in to call the commander and soon returned with a message.

"The lieutenant says you should come back tomorrow at eight a.m."

"Tomorrow is Monday and I will not be able to come because I have to go teach in the village and will not return until Friday.

"Wait here, I'll inform the *comandante*."

I waited in the street for his return.

"The lieutenant says you should present yourself here next Friday. And in the village you should report to the chief of the civil patrol."

"I will do so. Thank you."

I returned home feeling relieved. The danger was receding little by little, and my anxieties abated. I gathered the supplies I needed for my week in the village and lay down exhausted to listen to marimba music on my tape recorder.

That night, I'm not sure why, I fell asleep early. I did not even hear the barking of dogs during the night. I dreamt of being followed by strangers but I did not start awake in a sweat or walk in my sleep as I often had in the past.

I slept peacefully, like a child who does not know the meaning of the word, "danger."

At dawn I packed my shoulder bag with provisions for the week and left for the village. I looked for company along the way.

My wife and children were saddened by my departure, but I had to remain firm in my work and obligation. I walked along meditating on the sorrowful night I had spent on that same road when it was fraught with perils.

Dark clouds shadowed my memory of the past days. Only three days before, I had passed this way like a hog being led to slaughter, and now I was retracing my steps without ropes or other impediments. I felt master of myself and of the rolling hillsides. And suddenly on impulse, wanting the trees and even the rocks to share in my newborn happiness, I let out a cry of joy.

The four or five travelers accompanying me walked ahead without a word, their eyes fixed on the road as they dwelled on their own thoughts.

The road was drier because it had not rained the day before; some puddles remained in the shaded corners, but the main part was clear and easily traversed.

When we reached the summit of Pacayales hill, I paused at the promontory to gaze down on the smoking roofs of the desolate and sad village. It was seven a.m., and we ran into a few *campesinos* on their way up to till their fields in the high country.

Once more I grew sad and thoughtful, asking myself: "Why must the poor, the humble people always be the first ones to die?"

At eight sharp I reached the village. I saw a number of women washing their clothes and clay pots at the spring. They spoke softly, without the customary outbursts of laughter. When I passed near and greeted them, they looked at me curiously and said nothing.

A little farther ahead my students awaited me in the shade of the dense mango trees that stood next to the school. Their eyes and faces were lively and bright, as if shielded from the suffering of their elders.

I returned to my daily routine, tending to my classes as if nothing had happened. Three days passed swiftly, and on Thursday September 15th, we all celebrated together the anniversary of the National Independence.

In keeping with the program we had prepared earlier in the month, we celebrated with commemorative dramatic events and songs, read speeches and poems at the top of our voices, because on arriving I discovered that even the loudspeakers had been taken away by the military when they ransacked the village.

Silence reigned in the village during those days. No one commented on the tragedy, and even the civil defenders distrusted one another. They confined themselves to complying with the army's orders to run up the flag every morning at six and lower it at six every evening. And then taking turns guarding the entrances and exits to the village, they had to stand vigil all night. For the rest, everyone kept a hermetic silence.

PROTECTING MY LIFE

On that 15th of September, after the Independence Day celebrations were over, I packed my *morral* with fruits for my children and returned home, as the following day was an official holiday for public employees.

As I left, the marimba played behind me in the school patio, while the widows mourned their dead at the other end of town. The military had given orders to play the marimba on this great "Day of Liberty," even at the cost of neglecting the dead and wounded.

I could still hear the marimba as I climbed the eastern slope outside the village limits. I never fail to pause at this spot for a lingering glance down the narrow valley that the tranquil village of Tzalalá nestles in. Only this time, the closely huddled huts seemed like the cemetery of a remote and neglected country.

I was happy to arrive home and had time enough to take a stroll with my children to the center of town. I waited a short while longer before reporting to the barracks. A sergeant came and said,

"Come back tomorrow at eight a.m."

It was tedious and bothersome to be ordered around like some plaything, just to satisfy the whims of one's tormentors; but this was the only way I could show my innocence.

They wanted to wear me out and confuse me, but I refused to be put off by their repeated summons. I regarded them as simple conditions I had to keep to avoid more serious consequences.

I continued to report every day that week, until I returned to the village to teach. On the following Friday when I returned to town, I learned that two villagers were being held in the barracks after they were arrested by the civil patrol when they tried to cross the Mexican border with their families seeking refuge. They had been hooded and brought to town so no one would recognize them, but their identities were soon known to the townspeople. When I reported to the barracks on Friday afternoon I was told in grave tones to return the following morning at eight a.m.

"It's urgent," they warned me.

I rose early next day and went over in my head all the questions they could possibly ask me, as I was certain to be put through another interrogation.

I reported at eight sharp.

"Come inside and don't loiter in the street," I was scolded by the soldier standing guard.

I walked in slowly, feigning unconcern over the recent incidents in town. When the lieutenant arrived, he had a pencil and a sheet of paper in his hands. He sat down next to the door, with a Galil at his side – the first time I had seen him carry that weapon inside the barracks.

"This time we have something important to talk over," he said.

"May I know what about, *mi comandante?*"

"We have two men here I would like you to identify."

I leaned over and looked down at the two names written on his sheet of paper.

"You know these men, right?"

"Yes, they live in town, but I don't know them very well."

"What do they do?"

"I am not familiar with what they do, but I am certain they are *campesinos.*"

"But they claim to know you very well."

"Yes, perhaps. I live in town and everyone knows me."

I tried to avoid direct replies to his sly insinuations because I realized they were trying to incriminate me

110

with names and events the two captives had most likely not even confessed to.

As we spoke, the sergeant in charge of torture showed up with another sheet of paper. He flung me a venomous glance and announced in a loud voice to make certain that I heard:

"The two guerrillas have given the names of other companions of theirs. Here is the list."

He handed the commander a sheet of notebook paper, which had three columns of first names, without patronymics.

I would not swallow the bait. I figured out immediately that the sergeant had made up that list himself, as part of the dangerous game they were subjecting me to.

While the lieutenant read the list aloud, the sergeant watched me with a barely contained fury, as if wanting to tear me limb from limb with his loathsome expert torturer's hands.

The lieutenant directed a menacing look at me: "Ah, so it seems there are more guerrillas in your village; we will have to go down there one day soon, and finish them off."

"I don't know where all these lists are coming from. It was the same with the patrol that carried out the killings recently. They also brought a long list."

I had replied in my normal tone of voice, which appeared to stop my interrogators cold. If at that moment I had paled or reddened, or betrayed a tremor in my voice or the cuff of my trousers, I would have been dragged inside without need for further questions; but it did not turn out as they expected, and so the lieutenant tried another tack:

"And what has come of the conditions I set for you? Have you found out any names? I am waiting for a list of some sort from you."

"I've not been able to find out anything as yet," I said, to mollify him. But I knew I would never be capable of such monstrous cowardice.

"Keep in mind, then, that it was the condition under which I set you free. If you refuse to hold to it, that is another, serious matter. So think it over carefully and collaborate with us in denouncing anything suspicious."

"I'll see what I can do–give me time," I replied.

"All right, go on home and keep on reporting here as you've been doing."

"Thank you, *mi comandante*. Good bye."

I shook his hand and left at once, with a great satisfaction in my heart at having survived another horrible test with my life.

I returned innumerable times to report to the base commander, until he was relieved from his post. He was replaced by another lieutenant who had stored up in his being all the deadly poisons. I hesitated to present myself before him but finally had to do it to avoid intrigues and greater dangers.

"I know nothing of you," he said to me the first time, which was fine with me.

But some days later I learned he was carrying out a probe about me and my associations in town and in the village.

When I next reported to the commander, he said to me,

"You will have to report here without fail. And don't duck out on me because I'm not one to be fooled with, as you did with my predecessor. I just came from el Quiché and I know how to clean up towns infested by guerrillas."

"Be assured, I will comply with the order."

Around this time the school semester was coming to a close. I had written final evaluations for my pupils and prepared to fill out the end of term reports and lead the closing ceremonies. The last days of October resembled a sick burro reluctant to move a step. More corpses kept appearing in the outskirts of town, and machinegun volleys shattered the silence every night. The army infested the town with secret agents who sowed distrust and fear among the neighbors. Once more I began to fear the prospect of a late-night kidnapping; my sleep grew fitful and my dreams were stalked by nightly terrors.

With the rise to power of Efraín Ríos Montt, all remaining human rights were abolished, and the army became the sole arbiter over the lives of Guatemalans.

As the situation deteriorated day by day, I became convinced that I had to protect my life somewhere else, and so one dark night I fled with my wife and children in the firm expectation of returning when peace and tranquility will have returned to the beloved land of the quetzal.

Victor Montejo now lives with his wife and three children in Willimantic, CT. He is currently completing his doctoral studies in anthropology at the University of Connecticut. Born of Mayan parents in 1952 in rural Guatemala, he attended Maryknoll schools where he learned Spanish and received his teaching degree.

As his testimony indicates, Victor Montejo taught in a primary school in Guatemala where he witnessed the events told in this book. The name of the village has been changed to protect innocent people against reprisals. The events, however, occurred as recorded

In 1982 when Victor Montejo was in the United States working with Wallace Kaufman of Signal Books on his long poem *El Kanil: Man of Lightning,* the army and civil defense patrols began to harass his wife and children, and Victor learned that he was on a death list. Some North Americans in Guatemala helped his wife and children to leave the country legally. Soon after, a Victor Montejo Committee was set up in Lewisburg, Pennsylvania to provide support for the family, and Victor taught courses at Bucknell University, traveling from Bucknell to read and lecture at locations around the country. After serving as a research fellow at The West Branch School in Williamsport, Pennsylvania for six months, he accepted a fellowship in the doctoral program at SUNY to pursue his long-standing interest in anthropology, especially in Mayan hieroglyphics and folk tales, and after receiving his MA at SUNY-Albany he moved to Connecticut where he is completing his graduate studies.

GLOSSARY OF TERMS

adobe: a type of brick made with mud and straw and dried in the sun, used for building houses.

atole: drink made with boiled or toasted maize.

barrancos: steep cliff, precipice; deep ravine.

campesino: small farmer or field laborer.

chingada: motherfucker.

compañeros: persons who are good friends and who do the same work.

Coyá: Kanjobal Indian community bombed by the warplanes of President Lucas García in September of 1980 (200 people died).

Cuchumatanes: high mountains in western Guatemala.

garrote: thick club used for hitting or beating.

G-2: Secret unit of the army responsible for thousands and thousands of disappearances and deaths in Guatemala.

Huehuetenango: (abbrev. Huehue) City in western Guatemala and capital of the province by the same name.

kaibil(es): counter-insurgency soldiers named after the Mayan chief Kaibil who fought against the Spanish invaders during the Conquest.

maricones, heucos: insulting names for homosexuals.

marimba: Indigenous musical instrument, similar to a xylophone, made of wood.

milpa: seed-time, or land set aside for the cultivation of corn.

morral: small shoulder bag made of agave.

nixtamal: maize boiled in lime water to make tortillas.

patrón: boss of cotton, coffee, etc. plantations where the indigenous people work.

zopilote: scavenging bird of the vulture family.

Related titles available from Curbstone Press

Other books about Guatemala:

AFTER THE BOMBS, a novel by Arturo Arias, translated by Asa Zatz. A lyrical documentation of the 1954 coup in Guatemala, with zany humor and harsh insights into repression. $19.95cl. 0-915306-88-3 $10.95pa. 0-915306-89-1

GRANDDAUGHTERS OF CORN: Portraits of Guatemalan Women by Marilyn Anderson & Jonathan Garlock.
These photographs of Guatemalan women are accompanied by text that provides background for understanding the cultural as well as political realities in this turbulent country.
$35.00cl. 0-915306-64-6 $19.95pa. 0-915306-60-3

THE BIRD WHO CLEANS THE WORLD and other Mayan Fables by Victor Montejo; translated by Wallace Kaufman. This collection of Mayan fables presents an enjoyable introduction to this part of Mayan tradition and addresses the need to keep these traditions alive in spite of Guatemala's governmental pressure to the contrary. $22.95cl. 0-915306-93-X

Other testimonies:

MIGUEL MARMOL, by Roque Dalton; translated by Richard Schaaf. Long considered a classic testimony throughout Latin America, *Miguel Marmol* gives a detailed account of Salvadoran history while telling the interesting and sometimes humorous story of one man's life.
$19.95cl. 0-915306-68-9; $12.95pa. 0-915306-67-0.

Notes